T0087970

W. C. Whitfield's Mixed Drinks and Cocktails

An Illustrated, Old-School Bartender's Guide

Edited and Compiled by W. C. Whitfield
Illustrations by Tad Shell

Foreword by
Joaquín Simó

Skyhorse Publishing

Contents

Foreword

We are awash in the midst of a phenomenal second (or is it the third? fourth?!) Golden Age of the craft cocktail, and the Information Age is digitally aiding and abetting its rapidly democratizing flow of critical information in the way of ebooks, blogs, feeds, and boards. Yet we still find ourselves creeping around dusty bookstore stacks in search of some forgotten treasure that everyone else has happily overlooked. Cocktail books are a rather motley crew; not unlike the denizens who colorfully patronize the bars that have inspired great drinks, better times and worse decisions, but not always in that order. So why do we love these relics so much? Surely some of that answer must lie in the perfectly imperfect desire to combine what is eternally classic with what is currently cool. We love the glimpse back into another era—partly because some things are so implausibly different, and other things are so deliciously familiar.

Perusing classic cocktail books is like reading a diary written by long-dead ancestors, preserved under a dusty floorboard in their bedroom. Their diction and slang both delight and confound, their measurements and serving styles are equal parts specific and inscrutable, their ratios and formulae surely derived from ingredients and modifiers completely alien to our own. And yet we pore through them and read the recipes and coo over the illustrations, and then, just this one time, we make a drink we've never heard of, the contents of which we are slightly proud (and simultaneously slightly ashamed) to possess in our home bars, and give it the ole college try. To be fair, it usually does not end well. But that was hardly the point, was it? It's that knowing peek behind the curtain, behind the staid dusty official accounts of long forgotten social norms and customs, to the very fuel that ignited passions and theatrics from frontier saloons to speakeasy dancefloors to tiki huts. These books are snapshots of Gilded Age saloons, Parisian hotel bars, and suburban dinner parties. They're also instruction manuals for how to parse our ever-evolving tastes and gleefully snicker at our antecedents' clearly lacking sense of balance and sophistication. It's a good thing we've cleared all that up now. Ahem.

Some recipes collected here inspire wonder and awe—what kind of an epic night out must warrant a silver absinthe fizz (a rather overproof way to start your morning) as a day-after restorative tonic? Others remind us of how drink names can change over time: a "Dry Martini" from 1939 is extraordinarily wet by today's standards, while a "French Martini" used to mean a fairly dry gin martini but now refers to cloying confection comprised of vodka, pineapple, and Chambord. A modern bartender's equipment list is nearly identical to the bar kit listed here, though I would quibble with the author's assertion that shaken drinks are a listless sort to be avoided at all cost.

For the most part, the instructions given by the esteemed Mr. Whitfield are still perfectly valid. His voice is as cheeky as the illustrations accompanying the text, and it's clear that this amiable gent would be quite adept plying his time-honored craft behind any reputable craft cocktail bar today. Rather than making grand statements about definitive recipes, he urges his readers to try the various versions of the same drink he's collected to determine which is best for them. This sound advice is equally valid today. If most cocktail recipes were viewed more as gentle guidelines rather than hard-and-fast rules, people would be less intimidated by them and therefore emboldened to tweak proportions to suit their own tastes. So take this bartender's advice and learn the heart of the cocktails you love, rather than simply memorizing a recipe. Then open these books and find your new favorites amidst these hundreds of delightful drinks from a bygone age.

—Joaquín Simó
Partner, Pouring Ribbons, NYC
2012 TOTC Spirited Award for American Bartender of the Year

Just
COCKTAILS
A BARTENDER'S GUIDE

DECORATIONS BY TAD SHELL

Then to the Flowing Bowl
          did I adjourn
My lips the Secret Well
          of Life to learn,
And lip to lip it murmur'd -
          "While you live,
Drink! - for once dead you
          never shall return"

                    -OMAR KHAYYAM

A Real American Institution

We of this new world known as the United States of America are prone to yield the palm of cookery to the old world on the other side of the Atlantic.

As witness of this point take note of the fact that the famous chefs of our grandest hotels are almost invariably French, or Italian, or Spanish—usually of Latin origin, anyway. And every historic restaurant of gay New York and old New Orleans, almost without exception, gained its "place in the sun" because of the culinary skill of a foreigner.

But when it comes to the art of mixing drinks—well, that is a "horse of another color". In that field the new world tops the old—and how! The American bartender of the "Gay Nineties" was an institution. His fame spread to the four corners of the globe, and visitors to our shores from the continent bowed before his skill in concocting tempting mixtures of "liquid lightning". He was—and still is—in a class by himself. We may go to Europe for our chefs, but Europe comes to us for its bartenders.

Just why the American excels in this field is hard to say, but it is possibly for the same reason that we lead the world in inventive genius (an acknowledged fact). That reason is that we will "try anything once". We are not so tied by age-old conventions, are not so content to let custom rule us. We like to experiment in all fields, and so—when it comes to mixing drinks—we stop at nothing.

It is possible, of course, that many digestive tracts have been impaired by these experiments (we will concede that much to the abstainers), but the discovery that a smooth, mellow Manhattan cocktail will work miracles with a laggard appetite certainly makes up for such damages. And the soothing qualities of Creme de Cacao blended with "Cream de Cow" has done such wonders for those same digestive tracts that we can surely forgive some mistakes.

So here's to the Knight of the Brass Rail, and his many good deeds —quiet a few of which you will find on the following pages:—

USEFUL INFORMATION

MEASUREMENTS

1 DASH	1/3 TEASPOON
1 BARSPOON	1/2 TEASPOON
1 TEASPOON	1/3 TABLESPOON
1 TABLESPOON	1/2 FLUID OUNCE
1 PONY	1 FLUID OUNCE
1 JIGGER	1½ FLUID OUNCES
1 WINEGLASS	2 FLUID OUNCES

THE JIGGER ORIGINALLY HELD TWO OUNCES, BUT THAT WAS BEFORE PROHIBITION. IT HAS SINCE SHRUNK TO 1½ OUNCES.

THE USE OF A SHAKER IN MIXING COCKTAILS MEANS FAST MELTING ICE, AND A WEAKER, THINNER DRINK. IF YOU WANT POTENCY USE A MIXING GLASS AND A SPOON.

SUGAR IS NOT READILY SOLUBLE IN ALCOHOL, SO IT IS WELL TO KEEP ON HAND A SMALL AMOUNT OF SYRUP FOR SWEETENING DRINKS. THIS CAN BE MADE EASILY BY BOILING ONE POUND OF SUGAR IN ONE PINT OF WATER, AND CAN BE KEPT IN A BOTTLE.

COCKTAILS SHOULD BE SERVED IN CHILLED GLASSES. LET THEM STAND FILLED WITH SHAVED ICE WHILE THE DRINKS ARE BEING MIXED.

EQUIPMENT

STRAINER
MIXING GLASS
COCKTAIL SHAKER
LEMON SQUEEZER
LIME SQUEEZER
BARSPOON, LONG HANDLED
CORKSCREW WITH LONG SHANK
DASHER TOP, FOR BITTERS BOTTLES.
METAL JIGGER MEASURE
ICE BAG AND MALLET
WOODEN PESTLE

COCK TALES & COCKTAILS

The tale, or perhaps we should say the tales, of the cocktail, all go to prove that it is the most American of all mixed drinks.

Whether we take as our authority the story of the barmaid at the revolutionary tavern who tossed together a drink for some of Lafayette's officers, and as an afterthought snatched some feathers from a nearby rooster with which to spear the cherries, or whether we pin our faith to the legend of the buccaneers of the Spanish Main who stirred their concoctions of liquors looted from captured galleons with the plumage of West Indian Cocks, the important point is still this—the cocktail is All American, both in origin and name.

Their specific names are legion. There are more different kinds than any collection could ever contain. The most popular ones, those that are served at all bars, both private and public, number something like a score.

We have attempted to list these in the following group:—

OLD FASHIONED

1 JIGGER BOURBON
2 DASHES ANGOSTURA BITTERS
1/2 LUMP SUGAR
2 SPOONS WATER
STIR AND THEN ADD LUMP OF
ICE AND PIECES OF LEMON AND
ORANGE.

OLD FASHIONED (No. 2)

1 JIGGER RYE
1 DASH ANGOSTURA BITTERS
2 DASHES ORANGE BITTERS
1 LUMP SUGAR (CRUSHED)
1 LUMP OF ICE
DECORATE WITH LEMON AND
ORANGE.

MANHATTAN

1/2 RYE WHISKEY
1/2 ITALIAN VERMOUTH
1 DASH ORANGE BITTERS
SERVE WITH A MARASCHINO
CHERRY.

MANHATTAN (No. 2)

2/3 BOURBON
1/3 ITALIAN VERMOUTH
ADD A DASH OF ANGOSTURA
BITTERS AND A CHERRY.

GIN

1 JIGGER DRY GIN
3 DASHES BITTERS
1 TWIST LEMON PEEL

GIN (No. 2)

1 JIGGER GIN
3 DASHES GUM SYRUP
2 DASHES ANGOSTURA BITTERS
2 DASHES CURACAO
1 TWIST LEMON PEEL

MARTINI

1/2 TOM GIN
1/2 ITALIAN VERMOUTH
1 DASH ORANGE BITTERS
SERVE WITH A GREEN OLIVE.

FRENCH MARTINI

5/6 GIN
1/6 FRENCH VERMOUTH
TWIST OF LEMON PEEL ON TOP,
SERVE WITH A GREEN OLIVE.

DRY MARTINI

2/3 GIN
1/3 FRENCH VERMOUTH
1 DASH BITTERS
TWIST OF LEMON PEEL ON TOP,
SERVE WITH A GREEN OLIVE.

PRESIDENTE NEW ORLEANS

1 PONY RUM
1 PONY CURACAO
1 PONY FRENCH VERMOUTH
2 DASHES GRENADINE
SERVE WITH CHERRY AND
ORANGE PEEL.

PRESIDENTE CUBAN

1 JIGGER RUM
1 LIME (JUICE ONLY)
2 DASHES GRENADINE

ALEXANDER

1 PONY GIN
1 PONY CREME DE CACAO
1 PONY FRESH CREAM

ALEXANDER'S SPECIAL

1 PONY GIN
1 PONY CREME DE CACAO
1/2 LIME (JUICE ONLY)
1 DASH FRESH CREAM

MILLIONAIRE

1/3 JAMAICA RUM
1/3 APRICOT BRANDY
1/3 SLOE GIN
1 LIME (JUICE ONLY)
1 DASH GRENADINE

MILLIONAIRE (NO. 2)

2/3 DRY GIN
1/3 ABSINTHE (OR PERNOD)
1 WHITE OF EGG
1 DASH ANISETTE

BRANDY

1 JIGGER BEST BRANDY
2 DASHES BITTERS
1 DASH ITALIAN VERMOUTH
1 TWIST OF LEMON PEEL

DUBONNET

1/2 DUBONNET
1/2 DRY GIN

COGNAC

1/3 COGNAC
1/3 COINTREAU
1/3 LEMON JUICE

CHAMPAGNE

1/3 GLASS CRACKED ICE
1 LUMP SUGAR
2 DASHES ANGOSTURA BITTERS
1 SLICE ORANGE
CHAMPAGNE TO FILL THE FIVE
OUNCE CHAMPAGNE GOBLET WHICH
SHOULD BE USED. STIR GENTLY.

DIXIE WHISKEY

1 JIGGER WHISKEY
1 DASH ANGOSTURA BITTERS
2 DASHES CURACAO
4 DASHES CREME DE MENTHE
1/2 LUMP SUGAR

WHISKEY

1 JIGGER WHISKEY
4 DASHES SYRUP
1 DASH BITTERS

WHISKEY SOUR

1/2 RYE
1/2 LEMON JUICE
POWDERED SUGAR

SLOE GIN

2/3 SLOE GIN
1/3 PLYMOUTH GIN
1 DASH ORANGE BITTERS

BRONX

1 JIGGER DRY GIN
1/2 JIGGER FRENCH VERMOUTH
1/2 JIGGER ITALIAN VERMOUTH
ADD JUICE OF 1/4 ORANGE AND
SHAKE WELL. SERVE WITH SLICE
OF ORANGE.

BRONX EXPRESS

1/3 GIN
1/3 FRENCH VERMOUTH
1/3 ORANGE JUICE
1 DASH ABSINTHE

VERMOUTH

1 JIGGER FRENCH VERMOUTH
1 DASH ABSINTHE
1 DASH MARASCHINO
2 DASHES BITTERS
SERVE WITH A CHERRY

BACARDI

1 JIGGER BACARDI RUM
1/2 LIME (JUICE ONLY)
2 DASHES GRENADINE

ABSINTHE

1 PONY ABSINTHE
1 PONY WATER
2 DASHES BITTERS
3 DASHES BENEDICTINE

FANCY BRANDY

1 JIGGER FINE BRANDY
2 DASHES CURACAO
2 DASHES ANGOSTURA BITTERS
3 DASHES GUM SYRUP

—AND THEN THERE ARE
"PRETTY" COCKTAILS

Besides the group of cocktails listed in the preceding pages as the most popular (remember that you have a perfect right to disagree with this), there were quite a few in the old days that had the "call" with the fair sex, probably because the use of syrups of delicate color lent to most of them an aesthetic charm.

Of course, in this day of post-prohibition, the women-folk often pre-empt all the space at the bar, and take their liquor just as raw as the male of the species, so the pretty cocktails of the "Gay Nineties" are no longer classed as feminine in their appeal. Today they are favored by the man who likes his pre-dinner drink to have a sweeter tang to it, and perhaps not so much kick. Those who prefer to have the "hard liquor" taste disguised by fruit juices and syrups also favor this type of cocktail.

Some of the best known ones of both yesterday, meaning pre-prohibition times, and today, are given here:—

Pink Whiskers

1 PONY BRANDY
1 PONY FRENCH VERMOUTH
1/4 ORANGE (JUICE ONLY)
3 DASHES GRENADINE
1 DASH CREME DE MENTHE

Orange Blossom

1/3 TOM GIN
1/3 ITALIAN VERMOUTH
1/3 ORANGE JUICE

Paradise

1/3 GIN
1/3 APRICOT BRANDY
1/3 ORANGE JUICE

Coffee

2/3 PORT WINE
1/3 BRANDY
1 YOLK OF EGG
1 SPOON SUGAR

Creole

1/2 JIGGER BOURBON
1/2 JIGGER ITALIAN VERMOUTH
1 DASH BENEDICTINE
1 DASH MARASCHINO
1 TWIST LEMON PEEL

Magnolia Blossom

1/2 DRY GIN
1/4 FRESH CREAM
1/4 LEMON JUICE
1 DASH GRENADINE

White Rose

1 JIGGER DRY GIN
1/4 ORANGE (JUICE ONLY)
1 LIME (JUICE ONLY)
1/2 JIGGER MARASCHINO
1 WHITE OF EGG

Silver King

1 JIGGER DRY GIN
1/2 LEMON (JUICE ONLY)
1 WHITE OF EGG
2 DASHES SYRUP
2 DASHES ORANGE BITTERS

Bachelor's Bait

1 JIGGER DRY GIN
1 WHITE OF EGG
3 DASHES ORANGE BITTERS
3 DASHES GRENADINE

White Cargo

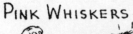

1 JIGGER DRY GIN
1 JIGGER VANILLA ICE CREAM
2 TEASPOONS WHITE WINE
SHAKE TILL THE ICE CREAM
    MELTS. NO ICE.

AMERICAN BEAUTY

1/4 BRANDY
1/4 FRENCH VERMOUTH
1/4 ORANGE JUICE
1/4 GRENADINE
1 DASH CREME DE MENTHE
TOP WITH A LITTLE PORT
   WINE

AROUND THE WORLD

1/2 PINEAPPLE JUICE
1/4 GREEN CREME DE MENTHE
1/4 DRY GIN

CAFE DE PARIS

1 JIGGER DRY GIN
3 DASHES ABSINTHE
1 TEASPOON FRESH CREAM
1 WHITE OF EGG

FIVE FIFTEEN

1 PONY CURACAO
1 PONY FRENCH VERMOUTH
1 PONY FRESH CREAM

BEAUTY SPOT

2/3 DRY GIN
1/3 GRENADINE
1 WHITE OF EGG

LADIES DELIGHT

1/2 JIGGER GIN
1/2 JIGGER ORANGE JUICE
1 DASH CURACAO
1 DASH LEMON JUICE
1/2 TEASPOON SUGAR

LOVE

1 JIGGER SLOE GIN
1 WHITE OF EGG
2 DASHES LEMON JUICE
2 DASHES RASPBERRY JUICE

ALEXANDER'S SISTER

1 PONY DRY GIN
1 PONY CREME DE MENTHE
1 PONY FRESH CREAM

JACK ROSE

2/3 APPLEJACK
1/3 GRENADINE SYRUP
1 LIME (JUICE ONLY)

BLUE DEVIL

1/2 DRY GIN
1/4 LEMON OR LIME JUICE
1/4 MARASCHINO
2 DASHES CREME DE YVETTE

POLLYANNA

3 SLICES ORANGE
3 SLICES PINEAPPLE
  (MUDDLE THESE THOROUGHLY)
1 JIGGER DRY GIN
1/2 JIGGER ITALIAN VERMOUTH
2 DASHES GRENADINE

CLOVER CLUB #1

1 JIGGER GIN
3 DASHES RASPBERRY SYRUP
1 WHITE OF EGG
1/2 TEASPOON SUGAR
1/2 LEMON (JUICE ONLY)
SHAKE WELL WITH ICE.

CLOVER CLUB #2

1 JIGGER GIN
1 DASH GRENADINE
1 WHITE OF EGG
1 LEMON (JUICE ONLY)

CLOVER LEAF

1 JIGGER DRY GIN
1 PONY ITALIAN VERMOUTH
1 WHITE OF EGG
1/2 LEMON (JUICE ONLY)
1 DASH GRENADINE
SERVE WITH A MINT LEAF.

WATERBURY

1 JIGGER BRANDY
1 WHITE OF EGG
1/2 LIME (JUICE ONLY)
1/2 TEASPOON POWDERED SUGAR
2 DASHES GRENADINE

COVINGTON

1/2 JIGGER BOURBON
1/2 JIGGER PORT WINE
1/4 LEMON (JUICE ONLY)
1/2 TEASPOON SUGAR
1 WHITE OF EGG
SERVE WITH SLICE OF PINEAPPLE

PINK LADY

1/3 GIN
1/3 LIME JUICE
1/3 APPLEJACK
2 DASHES GRENADINE

SNICKER

1 PONY DRY GIN
1/2 PONY FRENCH VERMOUTH
1 WHITE OF EGG
2 DASHES MARASCHINO
1 TEASPOON SYRUP
1 DASH ORANGE BITTERS.

HERE'S TO A LONG LIFE AND A MERRY ONE,
  A QUICK DEATH AND A HAPPY ONE,
A GOOD GIRL AND A PRETTY ONE,
  A COLD BOTTLE AND ANOTHER ONE.
                    – CLOVER CLUB TOAST

—NEXT COME THE
"EPICUREAN" COCKTAILS

There are also scores of cocktails—some authorities on "mixology" question their right to that classification—of which the countless array of tempting cordials form the base.

These are especially attractive to the epicure because they afford him such an endless variety in delicacy of taste. And why shouldn't they? Just stop to think that Benedictine, perhaps the oldest and best known liqueur is said to be a distillation of the choicest Cognac and over eighty varieties of spices and herbs, flowers and roots. And Chartreuse, another of the famous cordials, is supposed to have almost as many ingredients.

Whether the fact that both of these liqueurs were originally made in monasteries has anything to do with their goodness is beside the point. (Benedictine was actually brought to perfection by Friar Benedict, the founder of the order that bears his name). That they are good is beyond dispute, and they—as well as the countless other cordials that vie with them in the tempting tastes of Curacao, Kummel, Creme de Cacao, Cointreau, etc.—lend popularity to many drinks.

Some of these—we cannot even pretend that we are scratching the surface—are in the following list:—

BETWEEN THE SHEETS

1/3 Cointreau
1/3 Benedictine
1/3 Brandy

STINGER

1/2 White Creme de Menthe
1/2 Brandy

QUEEN ELIZABETH

1/3 Benedictine
1/2 Lime (juice only)
2/3 French Vermouth

BOHEMIAN GIRL

1 Jigger Creme de Cacao
1 Jigger Brandy
1 White of Egg
1/2 Lime (juice only)

DREAM

1/3 Curacao
2/3 Brandy
1 dash Absinthe

SNOWBALL

1/3 Gin
1/6 Creme de Violette
1/6 White Creme de Menthe
1/6 Anisette
1/6 Fresh Cream

PRINCE GEORGE

1/3 Grand Marnier
2/3 Bacardi
1/2 Lime (juice only)
Twist of Lemon peel.

KRETCHMA

2/5 Vodka
2/5 Creme de Cacao
1/5 Lemon Juice
1 dash Grenadine

WHITE LADY

2/3 Cointreau
1/6 Creme de Menthe
1/6 Brandy

XANTHIA

1/3 Cherry Brandy
1/3 Yellow Chartreuse
1/3 Gin

MAIDEN'S KISS

1/5 Creme de Roses
1/5 Curacao
1/5 Maraschino
1/5 Yellow Chartreuse
1/5 Benedictine

ANGEL'S KISS

1/4 CREME DE CACAO
1/4 BRANDY
1/4 CREME DE YVETTE
1/4 FRESH CREAM
POUR CAREFULLY, SO THAT
   INGREDIENTS DO NOT MIX,
   USING POUSSE CAFE GLASS.

YELLOW PARROT

1/3 BRANDY
1/3 YELLOW CHARTREUSE
1/3 ANISETTE

PING PONG

1/2 SLOE GIN
1/2 CREME DE YVETTE
1/4 LEMON (JUICE ONLY)
1 WHITE OF EGG

CHRYSANTHEMUM

1/2 BENEDICTINE
1/2 FRENCH VERMOUTH
3 DASHES ABSINTHE

SWISSESSE

1 JIGGER ABSINTHE
1/2 JIGGER ANISETTE
1 WHITE OF EGG

ST. PATRICK'S DAY

1/3 GREEN CREME DE MENTHE
1/3 GREEN CHARTREUSE
1/3 IRISH WHISKEY
1 DASH BITTERS
(ANY KIND EXCEPT ORANGE)

BENEDICTINE

1 PONY BENEDICTINE
1 PONY FRENCH VERMOUTH
1/2 PONY LIME JUICE

SWEET MARIE

1/5 BENEDICTINE
1/5 CURACAO
1/5 BRANDY
1/5 CHARTREUSE
1/5 FRESH CREAM

FORGET ME NOT

1/5 CHARTREUSE
1/5 MARASCHINO
1/5 BRANDY
1/5 CURACAO
1/5 FRESH CREAM

CONEY ISLE

1/4 CURACAO
1/4 CHARTREUSE
1/4 ABSINTHE
1/4 FRESH CREAM

ENCHANTED ISLAND
1 JIGGER BOURBON
1/2 JIGGER CREME DE CACAO
1 PONY FRESH CREAM
4 DASHES GRENADINE

TROPICAL
1/3 CREME DE CACAO
1/3 MARASCHINO
1/3 FRENCH VERMOUTH
1 DASH BITTERS

VIRGIN
1/3 FORBIDDEN FRUIT
1/3 WHITE CREME DE MENTHE
1/3 GIN
SHAKE WELL AND STRAIN.

CLOVEN HOOF
1/2 BRANDY
1/2 CREME DE MENTHE
1 DASH ABSINTHE

QUELLE VIE
1/3 KUMMEL
2/3 BRANDY

SIDE CAR
2/3 BRANDY
1/3 COINTREAU
1 DASH LIME JUICE

GYPSY
2/3 VODKA
1/3 BENEDICTINE
1 DASH BITTERS

DOLORES
1/3 CREME DE CACAO
1/3 CHERRY BRANDY
1/3 SPANISH BRANDY
1 WHITE OF EGG

WIDOW'S KISS
1/3 BENEDICTINE
1/3 PARFAIT D'AMOUR
1/3 YELLOW CHARTREUSE
1 WHITE OF EGG
   (FLOAT ON TOP)

MABEL BERRA
1/2 JIGGER SWEDISH PUNCH
1/2 JIGGER SLOE GIN
1/2 LIME (JUICE ONLY)

RUSSIAN

1/3 CREME DE CACAO
1/3 VODKA
1/3 DRY GIN

MERRY WIDOW

1/2 MARASCHINO
1/2 CHERRY BRANDY
STIR WELL WITH ICE AND
   SERVE WITH A CHERRY.

WIDOW'S DREAM

1 JIGGER BENEDICTINE
1 WHOLE EGG
SHAKE WELL, FLOAT ONE
   TABLESPOON CREAM ON
   TOP.

CASTLE DIP

1/2 WHITE CREME DE MENTHE
1/2 APPLE BRANDY
3 DASHES ABSINTHE

APPARENT

1 JIGGER CREME DE CACAO
1 JIGGER DRY GIN
1 DASH ABSINTHE

YELLOW DAISY

1 PONY GRAND MARNIER
1 PONY DRY GIN
1 PONY FRENCH VERMOUTH
1 DASH ANISETTE
SERVE WITH A CHERRY.

ROYAL SMILE

2 PONIES APPLE BRANDY
1 PONY DRY GIN
1/4 LEMON (JUICE ONLY)
2 DASHES GRENADINE

UNION JACK

1 PONY CREME DE YVETTE
2 PONIES DRY GIN
2 DASHES GRENADINE

JEWEL

1 PONY GREEN CHARTREUSE
1 PONY ITALIAN VERMOUTH
1 PONY DRY GIN
1 DASH ORANGE BITTERS

PANAMA

1 PONY CREME DE CACAO
1 PONY BRANDY
1 PONY FRESH CREAM

BLOCK & FALL

1/3 COINTREAU
1/6 ANISETTE
1/3 BRANDY
1/6 APPLEJACK

MORNING AFTER

2 JIGGERS ABSINTHE
1 TEASPOON ANISETTE SYRUP
1 WHITE OF EGG
1 DASH OF SODA (ON TOP)

DIANA

3/4 WHITE CREME DE MENTHE
1/4 COGNAC
FILL COCKTAIL GLASS WITH
    SHAVED ICE AND POUR THE
    ABOVE OVER IT.

PLUIE D'OR

1/3 VIELLE CURE
1/3 GIN
1/6 CURACAO
1/6 KUMMEL

GRENADINE

1/3 OXYGENE CUSENIER
1/3 WHITE CREME DE MENTHE
1/3 GIN
1 TEASPOON FRAMBOISE SYRUP
SHAKE WELL AND STRAIN.

NIGHT CAP

1/3 ANISETTE
1/3 CURACAO
1/3 BRANDY
1 YOLK OF EGG

AFTER SUPPER

1 PONY COGNAC
1 PONY CURACAO
4 DASHES LEMON JUICE

CANADIAN

1 JIGGER CURACAO
3 DASHES JAMAICA RUM
1/2 LEMON (JUICE ONLY)
1/4 TABLESPOON POWDERED SUGAR

BUTTON HOOK

1/4 WHITE CREME DE MENTHE
1/4 ABSINTHE
1/4 APRICOT BRANDY
1/4 COGNAC

CHOCOLATE

1/3 MARASCHINO
1/3 BLACKBERRY LIQUEUR
1/3 YELLOW CHARTREUSE
1 YOLK OF EGG

DIAMOND LIL

1/5 CURACAO
1/5 RUM
1/5 ABSINTHE
1/5 CREME DE YVETTE
1/5 GRENADINE

VOLSTEAD

1/3 SWEDISH PUNCH
1/3 RYE
1/6 ORANGE JUICE
1/6 RASPBERRY SYRUP
1 DASH ANISETTE

VALENCIA

2/3 APRICOT BRANDY
1/3 ORANGE JUICE
2 DASHES ORANGE BITTERS

ETHEL DUFFY

1 PONY WHITE CREME DE MENTHE
1 PONY BRANDY
1 PONY WHITE CURACAO

SMILE

1 JIGGER GRENADINE
1 JIGGER GIN
2 DASHES LEMON JUICE

ASTORIA QUEEN

1/4 BRANDY
1/4 CURACAO
1/4 MARASCHINO
1/4 FRESH CREAM

AMER PICON

1 JIGGER DRY GIN
1 PONY AMER PICON
3 DASHES GRENADINE

ULYSSES

1/3 CHERRY BRANDY
1/3 FRENCH VERMOUTH
1/3 COGNAC
1 ORANGE PEEL, SQUEEZED

LASKY

1 PONY SWEDISH PUNCH
1 PONY GRAPE JUICE
1 PONY GIN

SAY, WHY DID TIME,
  HIS GLASS SUBLIME,
    FILL UP WITH SAND UNSIGHTLY,
WHEN WINE HE KNEW,
  RUNS BRISKER THROUGH,
    AND SPARKLES FAR MORE BRIGHTLY?
      — MOORE

—THEN WE HAVE THE

"FAVORITE SONS"

Of course there are cocktails without end that were first mixed by or named after some celebrity, usually a native of the city or state where the drink had its birth. Often these do not have enough appeal to the palate to earn for them more than a local and sentimental popularity, but there are some exceptions to this rule.

For instance, the Sazerac cocktail was born in New Orleans, and christened after one of the daring blades of that historic city's Creole days, but it has come to be fairly popular from coast to coast. It has surely earned the right to head a group of cocktails that might be aptly designated the "favorite son" class, for they usually get the votes of only their home town constituency.

A call for one of these will almost invariably bring a blank stare to the face of your friend the bartender, but they are good and certainly deserving of more renown.

> If you don't find your especial pet in this group, turn to the back of the book and write it down on the blank page provided for just that purpose.

SAZERAC
1 JIGGER BOURBON OR SCOTCH
1 DASH ABSINTHE
1 DASH ITALIAN VERMOUTH
ADD A FEW DASHES OF
    PEYCHAND BITTERS.

CUBAN

2/3 BRANDY
1/3 APRICOT BRANDY
1/2 LIME (JUICE ONLY)

PALM BEACH

1/3 BACARDI RUM
1/3 GORDON WATER
1/3 PINEAPPLE JUICE

EVE'S APPLE

1/3 APPLEJACK
1/3 GRAPEFRUIT JUICE
1/3 GALDRIC PUNCH

MOUNTAIN
1 JIGGER BOURBON WHISKEY
1 DASH LEMON JUICE
1 DASH ITALIAN VERMOUTH
1 DASH FRENCH VERMOUTH
1 WHITE OF EGG

YELLOW RATTLER

1/4 DRY GIN
1/4 ITALIAN VERMOUTH
1/4 FRENCH VERMOUTH
1/4 ORANGE JUICE

DEAUVILLE
1/4 FINE COGNAC
1/4 APPLE BRANDY
1/4 COINTREAU
1/4 LEMON JUICE

ENGLISH ROSE
1/2 DRY GIN
1/4 COGNAC
1/4 FRENCH VERMOUTH
4 DASHES GRENADINE
1 DASH LEMON JUICE
RUB THE RIM OF GLASS WITH
    LEMON AND DIP IN POWDERED
    SUGAR.

BENNETT
1 WINEGLASS DRY GIN
1/2 LIME (JUICE ONLY)
1/2 TEASPOON POWDERED SUGAR
2 DASHES BITTERS

SEPTEMBER MORN
1 JIGGER RUM
1/2 LIME (JUICE ONLY)
3 DASHES GRENADINE
1 WHITE OF EGG

CATASTROPHE

1 JIGGER COGNAC
1/2 JIGGER APPLEJACK
1/2 JIGGER BENEDICTINE
2 DASHES ABSINTHE

RACQUET CLUB

1 WINEGLASS DRY GIN
1 PONY FRENCH VERMOUTH
1 DASH ORANGE BITTERS

OPERA

2 PONIES DRY GIN
1/2 PONY DUBONNET
1/2 PONY MARASCHINO

LADIES'

1 JIGGER BOURBON
2 DASHES ABSINTHE
3 DASHES ANISETTE
2 DASHES BITTERS
SERVE WITH A SLICE
    OF PINEAPPLE.

HOLLAND HOUSE

1 JIGGER DRY GIN
1/2 JIGGER FRENCH VERMOUTH
1/4 LEMON (JUICE ONLY)
4 DASHES MARASCHINO
1 SLICE PINEAPPLE

KNOCK-OUT

1 PONY ABSINTHE
1 PONY FRENCH VERMOUTH
1 PONY DRY GIN
1 TEASPOON WHITE CREME DE MENTHE
SERVE WITH A CHERRY

BOOSTER

1 JIGGER BRANDY
1 WHITE OF EGG
4 DASHES CURACAO
SERVE WITH GRATED NUTMEG
    ON TOP.

VANDERBILT HOTEL

1 JIGGER COGNAC
1/2 PONY CHERRY BRANDY
3 DASHES SYRUP
2 DASHES BITTERS

SAVOY TANGO

1 JIGGER SLOE GIN
1 JIGGER APPLEJACK

TWIN SIX

1 JIGGER DRY GIN
1/2 JIGGER ITALIAN VERMOUTH
1/4 ORANGE (JUICE ONLY)
1 WHITE OF EGG
1 DASH GRENADINE

WHIP

1 PONY BRANDY
1/2 PONY FRENCH VERMOUTH
1/2 PONY ITALIAN VERMOUTH
1 DASH ABSINTHE
3 DASHES CURACAO

BELMONT

2 PONIES DRY GIN
1 PONY RASPBERRY SYRUP
1 PONY FRESH CREAM

ALLIES

1 JIGGER DRY GIN
1 JIGGER FRENCH VERMOUTH
2 DASHES RUSSIAN KUMMEL

WHISKEY APPETIZER

1 JIGGER BOURBON
2 DASHES BITTERS
3 DASHES CURACAO

ZAZA

1 JIGGER DRY GIN
1/2 JIGGER DUBONNET
1 PIECE ORANGE PEEL

MINNEHAHA

1 JIGGER DRY GIN
1/2 JIGGER ITALIAN VERMOUTH
1/2 JIGGER FRENCH VERMOUTH
1/4 ORANGE (JUICE ONLY)

LEAVE IT TO ME

1 1/2 JIGGERS GIN
1 TEASPOON RASPBERRY SYRUP
1 TEASPOON LEMON JUICE
1 DASH MARASCHINO

POLO

2/3 DRY GIN
1/6 ORANGE JUICE
1/6 GRAPEFRUIT JUICE

PLANTER'S

1/2 JAMAICA RUM
1/4 LEMON JUICE
1/4 SYRUP

WASHINGTON'S
STIRRUP CUP

1 JIGGER BRANDY
1 JIGGER CHERRY BRANDY
1/2 LEMON (JUICE ONLY)

HAVE A HEART

1 JIGGER DRY GIN
1/2 JIGGER SWEDISH PUNCH
1/2 LIME (JUICE ONLY)
2 DASHES GRENADINE
SERVE WITH PINEAPPLE
    AND CHERRY.

DEPTH BOMB

1/2 Cognac
1/2 Apple Brandy
1 dash Lemon Juice
4 dashes Grenadine

KNICKERBOCKER

2/3 Dry Gin
1/3 French Vermouth
1 dash Italian Vermouth
1 twist Lemon Peel

SOUTH SIDE

1 jigger Dry Gin
1/2 Lemon (Juice only)
1 teaspoon Sugar
3 Mint Leaves

SOUTH SIDE (IRVIN COBB'S)

1 jigger Dry Gin
1 dash Curacao
1 Lime (juice only)
2 Mint Leaves
("On a warm day this South Side is as refreshing as the north side of a shade tree"
—Cobb)

SARATOGA

1 jigger Brandy
2 dashes Maraschino
2 dashes Pineapple Juice
1 dash Orange Bitters

MOULIN ROUGE

1/3 Italian Vermouth
2/3 Sloe Gin
1 dash Pernod

FLAMINGO

1 jigger Dry Gin
1/2 pony Brandy
1/2 Lime (juice only)
3 dashes Grenadine

HARRY LAUDER

1/2 Scotch Whiskey
1/2 Italian Vermouth
2 dashes Gum Syrup

NUMBER ONE

1 jigger Old Tom Gin
1 pony Italian Vermouth
1 twist Lemon peel

SMILER

1 jigger Dry Gin
1/2 jigger French Vermouth
1/2 jigger Italian Vermouth
1 dash Bitters
1 dash Orange Juice

FINE AND DANDY

1/2 DRY GIN
1/4 COINTREAU
1/4 LEMON JUICE
1 DASH BITTERS
SERVE WITH A CHERRY.

BILTMORE

1 PIECE FRESH PINEAPPLE
  (MUDDLED)
1 JIGGER DRY GIN
1/2 PONY ITALIAN VERMOUTH
1 DASH MARASCHINO
SERVE WITH A HAZEL NUT,
  PRESERVED IN MARASCHINO.

MALLORY

1/2 PONY COGNAC
1/2 PONY CREME DE MENTHE
1/2 PONY APRICOT BRANDY
2 DASHES ABSINTHE

OLD PAL

1/3 WHISKEY
1/3 CREME DE MENTHE
1/3 FRENCH VERMOUTH

NEVADA

1 JIGGER RUM
1/2 GRAPEFRUIT (JUICE ONLY)
1 LIME (JUICE ONLY)
1 DASH BITTERS
1 TEASPOON POWDERED SUGAR

DELMONICA SPECIAL

1 PONY GIN
1/2 PONY FRENCH VERMOUTH
1/2 PONY ITALIAN VERMOUTH
1 PONY BRANDY
3 DASHES ANGOSTURA BITTERS
1 TWIST LEMON PEEL

POPPY

2/3 DRY GIN
1/3 CREME DE CACAO

APPLE PIE

1/2 RUM
1/2 ITALIAN VERMOUTH
4 DASHES BRANDY
2 DASHES GRENADINE
4 DASHES LEMON JUICE

AFTER DINNER

1 JIGGER COGNAC
1 JIGGER CURACAO

SOUL KISS

1/3 WHISKEY
1/3 FRENCH VERMOUTH
1/6 ORANGE JUICE
1/6 DUBONNET

SHAMROCK

1/2 IRISH WHISKEY
1/2 FRENCH VERMOUTH
3 DASHES CHARTREUSE (GREEN)
3 DASHES CREME DE MENTHE
SERVE WITH AN OLIVE

CREOLE LADY

1 JIGGER WHISKEY
1 JIGGER MADEIRA WINE
3 DASHES GRENADINE
SERVE WITH TWO CHERRIES

JOCKEY CLUB

1 JIGGER DRY GIN
4 DASHES LEMON JUICE
2 DASHES CREME DE CACAO
1 DASH BITTERS

GOLDEN SLIPPER

1 JIGGER COGNAC
1 DASH YELLOW CHARTREUSE
1 YOLK OF EGG
FLOAT EGG YOLK. DO NOT
    SHAKE.

LITTLE DEVIL

1/6 LEMON JUICE
1/6 COINTREAU
1/3 RUM
1/3 DRY GIN

CHELSEA SIDE CAR

1 PONY COINTREAU
1 PONY DRY GIN
1 PONY LEMON JUICE

HAWAIIAN

2 PONIES DRY GIN
1 PONY PINEAPPLE JUICE
1 PONY CURACAO

MORNING

1 PONY BRANDY
1 PONY FRENCH VERMOUTH
2 DASHES CURACAO
2 DASHES ABSINTHE
2 DASHES ORANGE BITTERS
2 DASHES MARASCHINO

ROLLS ROYCE

1/4 FRENCH VERMOUTH
1/4 ITALIAN VERMOUTH
1/2 DRY GIN
1 DASH BENEDICTINE

INCOME TAX

1/2 DRY GIN
1/4 FRENCH VERMOUTH
1/4 ITALIAN VERMOUTH
1 DASH BITTERS
1/4 ORANGE (JUICE ONLY)

GOLDEN DAWN

1/4 APPLEJACK
1/4 APRICOT BRANDY
1/4 DRY GIN
1/4 ORANGE JUICE

GRAPEFRUIT

1 JIGGER DRY GIN
1 JIGGER GRAPEFRUIT JUICE
2 DASHES SYRUP

CLUB

1 JIGGER DRY GIN
3 DASHES RUM
3 DASHES ORANGE BITTERS
1 DASH GREEN CHARTREUSE

CLUB (NEW ENG-
LAND STYLE)

2/3 DRY GIN
1/3 ITALIAN VERMOUTH
SERVE WITH AN OLIVE.

CHAMPAGNE (AS
SERVED AT THE COP-
LEY PLAZA IN BOS-
TON)

1 LUMP SUGAR
2 DASHES ANGOSTURA BITTERS
   (SATURATE THE SUGAR WITH
   THIS)
1 PIECE LEMON PEEL
USE FIVE OUNCE STEM GLASS
   AND FILL WITH CHAMPAGNE.

CORNELL

1 JIGGER DRY GIN
1 WHITE OF EGG
3 DASHES MARASCHINO
2 DASHES LEMON JUICE

YALE

1 JIGGER DRY GIN
1/2 JIGGER FRENCH VERMOUTH
3 DASHES CREME DE YVETTE
1 DASH BITTERS

PRINCETON

1 JIGGER DRY GIN
1 JIGGER FRENCH VERMOUTH
2 DASHES LIME JUICE
SERVE WITH AN OLIVE.

HARVARD

1 JIGGER BRANDY
1 JIGGER ITALIAN VERMOUTH
1 DASH BITTERS
3 DASHES GRENADINE

PETER PAN

1/4 BITTERS
1/4 ORANGE JUICE
1/4 FRENCH VERMOUTH
1/4 DRY GIN

JACK RABBIT

1/3 DRY GIN
1/3 FRENCH VERMOUTH
1/6 BRANDY
1/6 COINTREAU

ABBEY

1 JIGGER DRY GIN
1/2 JIGGER ORANGE JUICE
1 DASH BITTERS
SERVE WITH A CHERRY.

ZAZARAC

1 JIGGER BOURBON
1 DASH RUM
1 DASH ANISETTE
1 DASH GUM SYRUP
1 DASH BITTERS
3 DASHES ABSINTHE

SIR WALTER (SWALTER)

1 PONY BRANDY
1 PONY RUM
1 TEASPOON GRENADINE
1 TEASPOON LEMON JUICE
1 TEASPOON CURACAO

HARLEM

2/3 DRY GIN
1/3 PINEAPPLE JUICE
3 DASHES MARASCHINO
SERVE WITH PINEAPPLE CUBES

PALL MALL

1/3 ITALIAN VERMOUTH
1/3 FRENCH VERMOUTH
1/3 DRY GIN
1 DASH ORANGE BITTERS
1 TEASPOON WHITE CREME DE MENTHE

BLUE TRAIN

1 JIGGER COGNAC
1 PONY PINEAPPLE JUICE
SHAKE WITH CRACKED ICE AND
   POUR INTO CHAMPAGNE GLASS.
   FILL WITH CHAMPAGNE, STIR
   GENTLY, AND SERVE AT ONCE.

WHITE WAY

1 WINEGLASS DRY GIN
1 PONY WHITE CREME DE MENTHE

POKER

1 JIGGER RUM
1 JIGGER ITALIAN VERMOUTH

EVERYBODY'S IRISH

1 JIGGER IRISH WHISKEY
6 DASHES GREEN CHARTREUSE
3 DASHES GREEN CREME DE MENTHE
1 GREEN OLIVE

DEMPSEY

1/2 DRY GIN
1/2 APPLE BRANDY
2 DASHES ABSINTHE
2 DASHES GRENADINE

COLD DECK
1/2 BRANDY
1/4 WHITE CREME DE MENTHE
1/4 ITALIAN VERMOUTH

WESTERN ROSE
1 JIGGER DRY GIN
1/2 JIGGER BRANDY
1/2 JIGGER FRENCH VERMOUTH
1 DASH LEMON JUICE

LA REGENCE
1/4 GIN
1/4 BRANDY
1/4 COINTREAU
1/4 ITALIAN VERMOUTH

WASHINGTON

1 PONY FRENCH VERMOUTH
1/2 PONY BRANDY
3 DASHES ANGOSTURA BITTERS
3 DASHES GUM SYRUP

KENTUCKY RIVER
3/4 BOURBON WHISKEY
1/4 CREME DE CACAO
4 DASHES PEACH BITTERS
1 TWIST LEMON PEEL

CASINO
1 1/2 JIGGERS DRY GIN
2 DASHES MARASCHINO
2 DASHES ORANGE BITTERS
2 DASHES LEMON JUICE
SERVE WITH A CHERRY.

APPLEJACK #1
1 JIGGER APPLEJACK
3 DASHES RASPBERRY SYRUP
3 DASHES GUM SYRUP

APPLEJACK #2
1 PONY APPLEJACK
1 PONY ITALIAN VERMOUTH
1 DASH ANGOSTURA BITTERS

BAMBOO
1/2 DRY SHERRY
1/2 ITALIAN VERMOUTH

QUAKER

1 PONY BRANDY
1 PONY RUM
1/2 PONY LEMON JUICE
1/2 PONY RASPBERRY SYRUP

THE COWBOY

2/3 SCOTCH
1/3 FRESH CREAM
ADD CRACKED ICE AND
    SHAKE WELL.

GRAY DAWN

1 JIGGER GIN
1 WHITE OF EGG
1 SPOONFUL WORCESTERSHIRE

BLACK EYE

1/2 SCOTCH
1/2 FRESH CREAM
3 DASHES CREME DE CACAO

ROB ROY

2/3 SCOTCH
1/3 ITALIAN VERMOUTH
1 DASH BITTERS

CHERRY BLOSSOM

1 PONY COGNAC
1 PONY CHERRY BRANDY
1 DASH CURACAO
1 DASH LEMON JUICE
1 DASH GRENADINE

APPETIZER

1 PONY DRY GIN
1 PONY DUBONNET
1/2 ORANGE (JUICE ONLY)

ALFONSO

1 PONY CREME DE CACAO
2 DASHES BITTERS
1 LUMP SUGAR
1 PIECE ICE
STIR GENTLY, POUR INTO
    CHAMPAGNE GLASS, FILL
    WITH CHAMPAGNE.

ELK'S OWN

1 JIGGER WHISKEY
1/2 JIGGER PORT WINE
1 WHITE OF EGG
1/2 LEMON (JUICE ONLY)
1 TEASPOON SUGAR
SERVE WITH A SLICE
    OF PINEAPPLE

LONE TREE

1/2 TOM GIN
1/4 ITALIAN VERMOUTH
1/4 FRENCH VERMOUTH

HONEYMOON

1 PONY BENEDICTINE
1 PONY APPLE BRANDY
1/2 LEMON (JUICE ONLY)
3 DASHES CURACAO

SKYROCKET

1 PONY WHISKEY
1 PONY SWEDISH PUNCH
1 PONY FRENCH VERMOUTH
1 DASH LEMON JUICE
1 DASH BITTERS

PARISIAN BLONDE

1 PONY JAMAICA RUM
1 PONY CURACAO
1 PONY FRESH CREAM

MAIDEN'S BLUSH

1 JIGGER DRY GIN
1 DASH LEMON JUICE
4 DASHES ORANGE CURACAO
4 DASHES GRENADINE

LIBERTY

1 JIGGER APPLEJACK
1/2 JIGGER JAMAICA RUM
1 DASH SYRUP

THIRD RAIL

1 PONY APPLEJACK
1 PONY RUM
1 PONY COGNAC
1 DASH ABSINTHE

SHRINER

1 PONY BRANDY
1 PONY SLOE GIN
2 DASHES BITTERS
2 DASHES GUM SYRUP
1 TWIST LEMON PEEL

SEVILLA

1 PONY PORT WINE
1 PONY JAMAICA RUM
1 WHOLE EGG
1/2 TEASPOON POWDERED SUGAR

LONDON

1 WINEGLASS DRY GIN
2 DASHES ORANGE BITTERS
2 DASHES SYRUP
2 DASHES MARASCHINO
1 TWIST LEMON PEEL

IMPERIAL

1 JIGGER FRENCH VERMOUTH
1 JIGGER DRY GIN
1 DASH MARASCHINO
1 DASH BITTERS

EYE OPENER

1 JIGGER RUM
1 YOLK OF EGG
1 TEASPOON POWDERED SUGAR
2 DASHES ABSINTHE
2 DASHES CURACAO
2 DASHES CREME DE CACAO

WEDDING BELLE

1 PONY DRY GIN
1 PONY DUBONNET
1/2 PONY CHERRY BRANDY
1/4 ORANGE (JUICE ONLY)

DU BARRY

2/3 DRY GIN
1/3 FRENCH VERMOUTH
1 DASH BITTERS
2 DASHES ABSINTHE
SERVE WITH SLICE OF ORANGE

FRANKENJACK

1 PONY DRY GIN
1 PONY FRENCH VERMOUTH
1/2 PONY COINTREAU
1/2 PONY BRANDY
SERVE WITH A CHERRY

BOSTON

1/4 DRY GIN
1/4 BRANDY
1/4 LEMON JUICE
1/4 GRENADINE

BLOODHOUND

1/2 DRY GIN
1/4 FRENCH VERMOUTH
1/4 ITALIAN VERMOUTH
2 OR 3 CRUSHED STRAWBERRIES

BOLERO

2/3 JAMAICA RUM
1/3 APPLEJACK
2 DASHES ITALIAN VERMOUTH

FLYING SCOTCHMAN

1/2 JIGGER SCOTCH WHISKEY
1/2 JIGGER ITALIAN VERMOUTH
1 DASH BITTERS
1 DASH SYRUP

SWISS FAMILY

2/3 BOURBON WHISKEY
1/3 FRENCH VERMOUTH
2 DASHES PERNOD
2 DASHES ANGOSTURA BITTERS

LOS ANGELES

1 JIGGER WHISKEY
1 LEMON (JUICE ONLY)
1 TEASPOON SUGAR
1 WHOLE EGG
1 DASH ITALIAN VERMOUTH

POLAR

1 PONY DRY GIN
1 PONY MARASCHINO
1/2 LEMON (JUICE ONLY)
1 WHITE OF EGG

BROKEN SPUR

2/3 PORT WINE
1/6 DRY GIN
1/6 ITALIAN VERMOUTH
1 YOLK OF EGG
1 TEASPOON ANISETTE

BRONX GOLDEN

1/2 DRY GIN
1/4 FRENCH VERMOUTH
1/4 ITALIAN VERMOUTH
1 TEASPOON ORANGE JUICE
1 YOLK OF EGG

BRONX SILVER

1 JIGGER DRY GIN
1/2 JIGGER FRENCH VERMOUTH
1 TEASPOON ORANGE JUICE
1 WHITE OF EGG

BULL DOG

1 JIGGER CHERRY BRANDY
1/2 JIGGER DRY GIN
1/2 LIME (JUICE ONLY)

ZULU

1/2 JIGGER DRY GIN
1/2 JIGGER CHERRY BRANDY
2 DASHES ANGOSTURA BITTERS

KENTUCKY COLONEL

1 JIGGER BOURBON WHISKEY
1/2 PONY BENEDICTINE
SERVE WITH A TWIST OF LEMON
   PEEL IN AN OLD FASHIONED
   GLASS.

NEW YORK

1 JIGGER WHISKEY
1 LIME (JUICE ONLY)
1/2 TEASPOON POWDERED SUGAR
2 DASHES GRENADINE
1 SLICE ORANGE PEEL

ADONIS

2/3 DRY SHERRY
1/3 ITALIAN VERMOUTH
1 DASH ORANGE BITTERS

SUNSHINE

1 PONY PINEAPPLE JUICE
1 PONY BACARDI RUM
1 PONY FRENCH VERMOUTH
1 DASH GRENADINE

TEMPTATION

1 JIGGER BOURBON
2 DASHES CURACAO
2 DASHES ABSINTHE
2 DASHES DUBONNET
1 PIECE ORANGE PEEL
1 PIECE LEMON PEEL

CORPSE REVIVER

1 JIGGER COGNAC
1/2 JIGGER APPLE BRANDY
1/2 JIGGER ITALIAN VERMOUTH

HOP TOAD

1 1/2 JIGGERS BRANDY
1/2 JIGGER LEMON JUICE

B.V.D.

1 PONY JAMAICA RUM
1 PONY DRY GIN
1 PONY FRENCH VERMOUTH

FLAG

1/2 JIGGER BRANDY
4 DASHES ORANGE CURACAO
POUR ONE TABLESPOON CREME DE
   YVETTE INTO 4 OZ. COCKTAIL
   GLASS, ADD THE ABOVE AFTER
   SHAKING, TOP WITH CLARET.

GILROY

1 PONY BRANDY
1 PONY DRY GIN
1/2 PONY FRENCH VERMOUTH
1/2 PONY LEMON JUICE
1 DASH ORANGE BITTERS

DAMN-THE-WEATHER

1 JIGGER DRY GIN
1/2 JIGGER ITALIAN VERMOUTH
1/2 JIGGER ORANGE JUICE
3 DASHES CURACAO

DEVIL'S

1 JIGGER PORT WINE
1 JIGGER FRENCH VERMOUTH
2 DASHES LEMON JUICE

T.N.T.

1 JIGGER WHISKEY
1 JIGGER ABSINTHE

UP TO DATE

1 JIGGER SHERRY WINE
1 JIGGER WHISKEY
2 DASHES GRAND MARNIER
2 DASHES BITTERS

DIXIE

1 PONY DRY GIN
1/2 PONY ABSINTHE
1/2 PONY FRENCH VERMOUTH
1/2 ORANGE (JUICE ONLY)

SEVENTH HEAVEN

1 WINEGLASS DRY GIN
1/2 PONY MARASCHINO
1/2 PONY GRAPEFRUIT JUICE
SERVE WITH A SPRIG OF FRESH
   MINT.

ECLIPSE

1/3 DRY GIN
2/3 SLOE GIN
2 DASHES LEMON JUICE
PUT ENOUGH GRENADINE IN
    GLASS TO COVER A RIPE
    OLIVE. SHAKE THE GIN,
    LEMON JUICE AND ICE
    WELL, THEN STRAIN IT
    GENTLY OVER THE GREN-
    ADINE SO THAT IT DOES
    NOT MIX.

GOOD TIMES

2/3 TOM GIN
1/3 FRENCH VERMOUTH
1 TWIST OF LEMON PEEL

AVIATION

1 JIGGER APPLEJACK
1/2 LIME (JUICE ONLY)
1 DASH ABSINTHE
1 BARSPOON GRENADINE

PICK-ME-UP

1 JIGGER COGNAC
1/2 LEMON (JUICE ONLY)
1 TEASPOON GRENADINE
STRAIN INTO CHAMPAGNE GLASS
    AND FILL BALANCE WITH
    CHAMPAGNE.

MAYFAIR

1/2 DRY GIN
1/4 BRANDY
1/4 ORANGE JUICE
1 DASH CLOVE SYRUP

ORIENTAL

1/2 JIGGER WHISKEY
1/4 JIGGER WHITE CURACAO
1/4 JIGGER ITALIAN VERMOUTH
1/2 LIME (JUICE ONLY)

RUM MANHATTAN

1 JIGGER RUM
1/2 JIGGER ITALIAN VERMOUTH
1 DASH BITTERS

CHINESE

2/3 JAMAICA RUM
1/3 GRENADINE
1 DASH BITTERS
3 DASHES MARASCHINO
3 DASHES CURACAO

BRANDY BLAZER

2 JIGGERS BRANDY
1 LUMP SUGAR
1 PIECE ORANGE PEEL
1 PIECE LEMON PEEL
USE HOT WHISKEY GLASS,
    STIR, AND LIGHT WITH
    A MATCH.

SHANGHAI

1 JIGGER JAMAICA RUM
1 PONY LEMON JUICE
4 DASHES ANISETTE
2 DASHES GRENADINE

TIPPERARY

1 PONY IRISH WHISKEY
1 PONY GREEN CHARTREUSE
1 PONY ITALIAN VERMOUTH

THUNDER CLAP

1 PONY BRANDY
1 PONY DRY GIN
1 PONY BOURBON

PLAZA

1/3 DRY GIN
1/3 FRENCH VERMOUTH
1/3 ITALIAN VERMOUTH
1 SLICE PINEAPPLE

FAIR & WARMER

2 PONIES JAMAICA RUM
1 PONY ITALIAN VERMOUTH
2 DASHES CURACAO

FALLEN ANGEL

1 JIGGER DRY GIN
1/2 LIME (JUICE ONLY)
2 DASHES CREME DE MENTHE
1 DASH BITTERS
SERVE WITH A CHERRY.

SAUCY SUE

1 WINEGLASS APPLEJACK
2 DASHES BRANDY
1 DASH ABSINTHE

HOFFMAN HOUSE

2 PONIES DRY GIN
1 PONY FRENCH VERMOUTH
2 DASHES ORANGE BITTERS
SERVE WITH OLIVE

KISS IN THE DARK

1 PONY CHERRY LIQUEUR
1 PONY GIN
1 PONY FRENCH VERMOUTH

BRANDY GUMP

1 JIGGER BRANDY
1 LEMON (JUICE ONLY)
2 DASHES GRENADINE

COMMODORE

1/3 BOURBON
1/3 CREME DE CACAO
1/3 LEMON JUICE
1 DASH GRENADINE
SERVE IN CHAMPAGNE GLASS

PINK ELEPHANT

2/3 DRY GIN
1/3 ITALIAN VERMOUTH
1 WHITE OF EGG
SHAKE WELL.

ASTORIA

2/3 SLOE GIN
1/3 FRENCH VERMOUTH
1 DASH ORANGE BITTERS

SLOE BERRY

1 JIGGER SLOE GIN
1 DASH ORANGE BITTERS

SHERRY

1 1/2 JIGGERS SHERRY
1 DASH ORANGE BITTERS
1 DASH ANGOSTURA BITTERS

MODERN #1

19 20's

1 JIGGER SCOTCH WHISKEY
2 DASHES LEMON JUICE
1 DASH ABSINTHE
2 DASHES JAMAICA RUM
1 DASH ORANGE BITTERS

MODERN #2

19 30's

2/3 SLOE GIN
1/3 SCOTCH WHISKEY
1 DASH PERNOD
1 DASH GRENADINE
1 DASH ORANGE BITTERS

FUTURITY

1/2 ITALIAN VERMOUTH
1/2 SLOE GIN
1 DASH ANGOSTURA BITTERS
2 DASHES GRENADINE

GOOD FELLOW

1/2 BOURBON WHISKEY
1/2 ITALIAN VERMOUTH
1 DASH ANGOSTURA BITTERS

MARCONI

2/3 APPLE BRANDY
1/3 ITALIAN VERMOUTH

BRIDAL

2/3 DRY GIN
1/3 ITALIAN VERMOUTH
1 DASH ORANGE BITTERS
1 DASH MARASCHINO
    ORANGE PEEL ON TOP.

FARMER'S

1/2 DRY GIN
1/4 ITALIAN VERMOUTH
1/4 FRENCH VERMOUTH
3 DASHES ANGOSTURA BITTERS

WARD EIGHT

1/2 BOURBON WHISKEY
1/4 LEMON JUICE
1/4 ORANGE JUICE
1 DASH GRENADINE

MIAMI

1 PONY RUM
1 PONY COINTREAU
3 DASHES LEMON JUICE

ROCK & RYE

1 JIGGER ROCK AND RYE
1 PONY PORT WINE
1 DASH ANGOSTURA BITTERS
1 DASH LIME JUICE

BOBBY BURNS

3/4 SCOTCH WHISKEY
1/4 ITALIAN VERMOUTH
2 DASHES BENEDICTINE

WALDORF

1/3 JIGGER RYE
1/3 JIGGER ABSINTHE
1/3 JIGGER ITALIAN VERMOUTH
1 DASH BITTERS

BOMBAY

1 JIGGER BRANDY
1/2 JIGGER FRENCH VERMOUTH
1/2 JIGGER ITALIAN VERMOUTH
1 DASH ABSINTHE
2 DASHES CURACAO

WEEP NO MORE

1 JIGGER COGNAC
1 JIGGER DUBONNET
1/2 LIME (JUICE ONLY)
1 DASH MARASCHINO

LEAP YEAR

1 WINEGLASS DRY GIN
1/2 PONY GRAND MARNIER
1/2 PONY ITALIAN VERMOUTH
1 DASH LEMON JUICE

CHAUNCEY

1/4 RYE
1/4 GIN
1/4 BRANDY
1/4 ITALIAN VERMOUTH
1 DASH ORANGE BITTERS

MAIDEN'S PRAYER

1 JIGGER DRY GIN
1 DASH COINTREAU
1 DASH LEMON JUICE
1 DASH ORANGE JUICE

CORONATION

1/3 Italian Vermouth
1/3 French Vermouth
1/3 Applejack
1 dash Apricot Brandy

EARTHQUAKE

1/3 Gin
1/3 Absinthe
1/3 Scotch

BLUE MOON

2/3 Gin
1/3 French Vermouth
1 dash Orange Bitters
1 dash Creme Yvette

MONTE CRISTO

2/3 Cognac
1/3 Italian Vermouth

GOLDEN GATE

1/4 Gin
3/4 Orange Ice
Shake until melted

WEDDING BELLS

1/6 Cherry Brandy
1/6 Orange Juice
1/3 Gin
1/3 Dubonnet

WARDAY'S

1 teaspoon Yellow Chartreuse
1/3 Applejack
1/3 Italian Vermouth
1/3 Gin

JAPALAC

1 jigger Rye
1 jigger French Vermouth
1/4 Orange (juice only)
1 dash Raspberry Syrup

LIBERAL

1/2 Rye
1/2 Italian Vermouth
3 dashes Amer Picon
1 dash Orange Bitters

BLACK HAWK

1/2 Rye
1/2 Sloe Gin

TANGO

1/2 Applejack
1/2 Sloe Gin

OASIS

2 ponies Sloe Gin
1 pony Grapefruit Juice
  (unsweetened)

JOURNALIST

1 WINEGLASS DRY GIN
1/2 PONY FRENCH VERMOUTH
1/2 PONY ITALIAN VERMOUTH
2 DASHES LEMON JUICE
2 DASHES CURACAO
1 DASH BITTERS

BLOOD AND SAND

1 PONY SCOTCH WHISKEY
1 PONY CHERRY BRANDY
1 PONY ITALIAN VERMOUTH
1/4 ORANGE (JUICE ONLY)

GUARD'S

2 PONIES DRY GIN
1 PONY ITALIAN VERMOUTH
2 DASHES CURACAO
SERVE WITH A CHERRY

SAXON

1 JIGGER JAMAICA RUM
1/2 LIME (JUICE ONLY)
1 PIECE ORANGE PEEL
2 DASHES GRENADINE

FRENCH ROSE

1 JIGGER GIN
1/2 JIGGER FRENCH VERMOUTH
1/2 JIGGER CHERRY LIQUEUR

SLOPPY JOE'S

1 JIGGER PINEAPPLE JUICE
1/2 JIGGER COGNAC
1/2 JIGGER PORT WINE
1 DASH CURACAO
1 DASH GRENADINE

CLASSIC

1 JIGGER BRANDY
1/2 PONY CURACAO
1/2 PONY MARASCHINO
1/2 PONY LEMON JUICE
FROST RIM OF GLASS WITH SUGAR

FOX RIVER

1 JIGGER BOURBON
1/2 PONY CREME DE CACAO
4 DASHES BITTERS
ADD PIECE OF ICE, STIR WELL.

GREEN ROOM

1 JIGGER FRENCH VERMOUTH
1/2 JIGGER BRANDY
2 DASHES CURACAO

BIG BAD WOLF

2/3 BRANDY
1/3 CURACAO
1 YOLK OF EGG
1 SPOONFUL GRENADINE

PREAKNESS

1/3 Italian Vermouth
2/3 Rye Whiskey
1 dash Angostura Bitters
2 dashes Benedictine
1 twist Lemon Peel

EMERALD ISLE

1 jigger Dry Gin
1 teaspoon Creme de Menthe
3 dashes Bitters

X.Y.Z.

1/2 Jamaica Rum
1/4 Cointreau
1/4 Lemon Juice

BALTIMORE BRACER

1/2 Anisette
1/2 Cognac
1 White of Egg

ZANZIBAR

1/3 Dry Gin
1/3 French Vermouth
1/3 Lemon Juice
1 dash Gum Syrup
1 dash Orange Bitters

COLONIAL

2/3 Dry Gin
1/3 Grapefruit Juice
3 dashes Maraschino

SANTIAGO

2 dashes Grenadine
2 dashes Lemon Juice
1 jigger Rum

AFFINITY

1/3 Scotch Whiskey
1/3 French Vermouth
1/3 Italian Vermouth

WALLICK

1 jigger Gin
1 jigger French Vermouth
3 dashes Curacao

TAILSPIN

1 pony Green Chartreuse
1 pony Italian Vermouth
1 pony Gin
1 dash Orange Bitters
1 twist Lemon Peel
Serve with a cherry
     or olive.

FROTH BLOWER

1 jigger Gin
1 White of Egg
1 teaspoon Grenadine

CAMERON'S KICK

1/3 SCOTCH WHISKEY
1/3 IRISH WHISKEY
1/6 LEMON JUICE
1/6 ORANGE BITTERS

CABARET

1 JIGGER DRY GIN
2 DASHES BITTERS
2 DASHES FRENCH VERMOUTH
2 DASHES BENEDICTINE
SERVE WITH A CHERRY

CARUSO

1/3 DRY GIN
1/3 FRENCH VERMOUTH
1/3 GREEN CREME DE MENTHE

BRAZIL

1/2 FRENCH VERMOUTH
1/2 SHERRY
1 DASH BITTERS
1 DASH ABSINTHE

BRAINSTORM

1 JIGGER IRISH WHISKEY
1 CUBE OF ICE
2 DASHES FRENCH VERMOUTH
2 DASHES BENEDICTINE
1 PIECE ORANGE PEEL
SERVE WITH BARSPOON IN OLD
FASHIONED GLASS.

ALASKA

3/4 DRY GIN
1/4 YELLOW CHARTREUSE
2 DASHES ORANGE BITTERS

BURMUDA ROSE

1/2 DRY GIN
1/4 BRANDY
1/4 GRENADINE

BARBARY COAST

1/4 DRY GIN
1/4 SCOTCH WHISKEY
1/4 CREME DE CACAO
1/4 FRESH CREAM

BOX CAR

1/2 JIGGER GIN
1/2 JIGGER COINTREAU
1/2 LIME (JUICE ONLY)
1 WHITE OF EGG
1 DASH GRENADINE
SERVE IN GLASS WITH
FROSTED RIM.

TURF

1/2 GIN
1/2 FRENCH VERMOUTH
2 DASHES ORANGE BITTERS
2 DASHES ABSINTHE
2 DASHES MARASCHINO
SERVE WITH AN OLIVE

BROWN UNIVERSITY

1/2 BOURBON WHISKEY
1/2 FRENCH VERMOUTH
2 DASHES ORANGE BITTERS

PAN AMERICAN

1 JIGGER RYE
1/2 LEMON (JUICE ONLY)
3 DASHES SYRUP

HONOLULU

1/3 BOURBON
1/3 FRENCH VERMOUTH
1/3 ITALIAN VERMOUTH

GREEN DRAGON

1/2 DRY GIN
1/4 CREME DE MENTHE
1/8 KUMMEL
1/8 LEMON JUICE
4 DASHES ORANGE BITTERS

SALOME

1/3 FRENCH VERMOUTH
1/3 DRY GIN
1/3 DUBONNET

HAVANA

2/3 PINEAPPLE JUICE
1/3 RUM
2 DASHES LEMON JUICE

THUNDER & LIGHTNING

1 JIGGER COGNAC
1 YOLK OF EGG
1 TEASPOON POWDERED SUGAR

CUPID

1 JIGGER SHERRY
1 FRESH EGG
1 TEASPOON SUGAR
ADD NUTMEG IN SERVING

CRYSTAL SLIPPER

3/4 DRY GIN
1/4 CREME DE YVETTE
2 DASHES ORANGE BITTERS

HURRICANE

1/3 WHISKEY
1/3 DRY GIN
1/3 CREME DE MENTHE
1/2 ORANGE (JUICE ONLY)

COCKTAILS OF THE
"GAY NINETIES"

The recipes in this group will be of particular interest to the younger set, who are eternally being reminded of the "good old days" before prohibition. With these they may draw their own conclusions as to the relative merits of the drinks of yesterday and today.

Father and grandfather, (not mother, she drank tea and lemonade) will still argue that "those were the days" of real drinking, and proper drinking, too. Dad will maintain, if given half a chance, that the gentleman of the waning years of the nineteenth century knew his liquor and how to take it—and when to stop. And he will tell you that the whiskies and brandies of then were better than can be had today.

Without attempting to take any sides in this matter it is interesting to note that the kinds of cocktails served in the "Gay Nineties" were definitely fewer in number. There were less than forty variations of the Great American Drink served commonly at that time. Of course many of the "stand-bys" of today were being mixed then, notably the Manhattan and the Old Fashioned, but the Martini of now seems to have originally been known as the Martinez. At least in the recipe lists of the old days there appears the Martinez, and it is described "same as Manhattan, substituting Gin for Whiskey".

Such familiar acquaintances of these days as the Bronx, the Side Car, the Orange Blossom, and the Stinger are not to be found in the old books. On the other hand, we do come across many that are definitely dated by their names, like the Trilby and the Buster Brown, unheard of today.

Judging by the recipes in the old books, the changes made in the concoction of cocktails of the same names today are not exactly radical. In fact the differences are trifling in the main, still we know that just a dash of this or that can mean a lot to the palate.

At any rate, it was our thought that you might like to study these cocktails of our fathers, these mixtures of the "Gay Nineties", so here is a fairly complete list of them.

BLACKTHORNE

1/2 WINEGLASS SLOE GIN
1/2 WINEGLASS FRENCH VERMOUTH
1 TEASPOON SYRUP
2 DASHES LEMON JUICE
2 DASHES ORANGE BITTERS
1 DASH ANGOSTURA BITTERS

ABSINTHE

1 PONY ABSINTHE
1 WINEGLASS WATER
  (POUR IN SLOWLY)
1 TEASPOON SYRUP
2 DASHES ANGOSTURA BITTERS

GOLDEN BELL

1 JIGGER SHERRY
1 PONY VERMOUTH
3 DASHES ORANGE BITTERS
1 PIECE ORANGE PEEL

CHAMPAGNE

1 SMALL LUMP ICE
1 LUMP SUGAR
2 DASHES ANGOSTURA BITTERS
1 TWIST LEMON PEEL
CHAMPAGNE TO FILL GLASS

CLUB

3/4 JIGGER OLD BRANDY
2 DASHES MARASCHINO
2 DASHES PINEAPPLE JUICE
2 DASHES BITTERS
MIX WITH ICE AND STRAIN, DRESS
WITH STRAWBERRIES AND TWIST OF
LEMON PEEL, ADD DASH OF
CHAMPAGNE.

DERONDA

2/3 PLYMOUTH GIN
1/3 CALISAYA

EXPRESS

1 PONY SCOTCH
1 PONY ITALIAN VERMOUTH
2 DROPS SYRUP
3 DASHES ORANGE BITTERS

LONE TREE

1 WINEGLASS TOM GIN
1 PONY ITALIAN VERMOUTH

OLD SPORT

1/2 JIGGER RYE
1/2 JIGGER SHERRY
2 TEASPOONS SYRUP
1 TEASPOON PINEAPPLE SYRUP
2 DASHES ORANGE BITTERS
1 DASH PEYSCHAND'S BITTERS
RINSE COCKTAIL GLASS WITH
ABRICOTINE. STRAIN INTO SAME,
DASH WITH SELTZER AND DRESS
WITH FRUIT.

BUSTER BROWN

1 JIGGER WHISKEY
2 DASHES LEMON JUICE
1 TEASPOON SYRUP
2 DASHES ORANGE BITTERS

BRANDY

1 WINEGLASS FINE BRANDY
2 DASHES ANGOSTURA BITTERS
1 TEASPOON SYRUP
1 TWIST LEMON PEEL

COUNTRY

1 JIGGER RYE
2 DASHES ANGOSTURA BITTERS
2 DASHES ORANGE BITTERS
1 PIECE LEMON PEEL

GOLF LINKS

1/2 WINEGLASS RYE
1/2 WINEGLASS SWEET CATAWBA
2 DASHES LEMON JUICE
1 TEASPOON SYRUP
2 DASHES ORANGE BITTERS
1 DASH ANGOSTURA BITTERS
1 DASH RUM
RINSE COCKTAIL GLASS WITH
ABRICOTINE, STRAIN INTO SAME,
DASH WITH APOLLINARIS AND
DRESS WITH FRUIT.

GIN

1 WINEGLASS GIN
1 TEASPOON SYRUP
2 DASHES ORANGE BITTERS
1 DASH ANGOSTURA BITTERS
1 PIECE LEMON PEEL

DIXIE WHISKEY

1 JIGGER WHISKEY
1 LUMP SUGAR (DISSOLVED)
1 DASH LEMON JUICE
2 DASHES ANGOSTURA BITTERS
1 DASH CURACAO
5 DROPS CREME DE MENTHE

DUPLEX

1/2 ITALIAN VERMOUTH
1/2 FRENCH VERMOUTH
3 DASHES ORANGE BITTERS
3 DASHES ACID PHOSPHATE

FANCY BRANDY

1 JIGGER FINE BRANDY
1 DASH ORANGE BITTERS
2 DASHES ANGOSTURA BITTERS
3 DASHES MARASCHINO
MOISTEN RIM OF GLASS WITH
PIECE OF LEMON AND DIP IN
POWDERED SUGAR.

HARVARD

1 1/2 PONIES BRANDY
1 PONY ITALIAN VERMOUTH
3 DASHES ANGOSTURA BITTERS
1 DASH GUM SYRUP
STRAIN INTO A COCKTAIL GLASS,
FILL WITH SELTZER AND SERVE
QUICKLY.

MARTINEZ

1/2 GIN
1/2 ITALIAN VERMOUTH
1 DASH ANGOSTURA BITTERS
1/2 BARSPOON SUGAR
1 TWIST LEMON PEEL

MANHATTAN

1/2 WHISKEY
1/2 ITALIAN VERMOUTH
1 DASH ANGOSTURA BITTERS
1/2 BARSPOON SUGAR
1 TWIST LEMON PEEL

METROPOLE

3/4 JIGGER BRANDY
1/2 JIGGER FRENCH VERMOUTH
2 DASHES GUM SYRUP
1 DASH ORANGE BITTERS
2 DASHES ANGOSTURA BITTERS

OLD FASHIONED

1 LUMP SUGAR
1 DASH SELTZER
(CRUSH SUGAR WITH MUDDLER)
1 CUBE ICE
1 JIGGER WHISKEY
1 DASH ORANGE BITTERS
1 DASH ANGOSTURA BITTERS
1 PIECE LEMON PEEL
STIR GENTLY AND SERVE WITH
A SPOON.

OLD TOM GIN

1 WINEGLASS OLD TOM GIN
3 DASHES GUM SYRUP
2 DASHES ANGOSTURA BITTERS
2 DASHES CURACAO
1 TWISTED LEMON PEEL

SARATOGA

1 PONY BRANDY
1 PONY WHISKEY
1 PONY VERMOUTH
1 SLICE LEMON

TRILBY

2/3 WHISKEY
1/3 CALISAYA
3 DASHES ORANGE BITTERS
3 DASHES ACID PHOSPHATE

IRISH

1 WINEGLASS IRISH WHISKEY
1 PONY ITALIAN VERMOUTH
3 DASHES ORANGE BITTERS
2 DASHES ACID PHOSPHATE

TUXEDO

3/4 JIGGER TOM GIN
1/2 JIGGER ITALIAN VERMOUTH
1 BARSPOON SHERRY WINE
1 DASH ANGOSTURA BITTERS

WHISKEY

1 JIGGER WHISKEY
1 LUMP SUGAR (DISSOLVED)
1 DASH LEMON JUICE
2 DASHES ANGOSTURA BITTERS

WHISKEY (NEW YORK)

1 JIGGER WHISKEY
1/2 JIGGER ITALIAN VERMOUTH
1/2 TEASPOON SHERRY WINE
2 DASHES ANGOSTURA BITTERS
1 TWIST LEMON PEEL

VERMOUTH

1 1/2 PONIES FRENCH VERMOUTH
3 DASHES ANGOSTURA BITTERS
2 DASHES GUM SYRUP

STAR

3/4 JIGGER APPLE BRANDY
1/2 JIGGER ITALIAN VERMOUTH
2 DASHES GUM SYRUP
3 DASHES ORANGE BITTERS
1 TWIST LEMON PEEL

RISING SUN

1 WINEGLASS BRANDY
1 TEASPOON CURACAO
1 TEASPOON PINEAPPLE SYRUP
3 DASHES ANGOSTURA BITTERS
2 DASHES MARASCHINO
1 TWIST LEMON PEEL

REMEMBER—
THESE COCKTAILS WERE THE VOGUE LONG BEFORE PROHIBITION, SO
WHEN A RECIPE CALLS FOR A JIGGER IT MEANS TWO FULL OUNCES.

"LET ME PLAY THE FOOL, WITH MIRTH AND LAUGHTER LET OLD
WRINKLES COME; AND LET MY LIVER RATHER HEAT WITH WINE,
THAN MY HEART COOL WITH MORTIFYING GROANS."
— SHAKESPEARE

HERE'S HOW

MIXED DRINKS

A Modern Art—This Mixing Of Drinks

THE art of mixing drinks—and make no mistake, it is an art—can be definitely fixed as a development of this very modern age of ours. To be sure, they did throw together various concoctions of spirits in days long gone by, as far back as the Middle Ages and even earlier than that. Some of these, like the Wassail Bowl and the Huckle-By-Butt that are famed in both the fact and fiction of the Crusades, are even yet mixed on gay and festive occasions in "Merrie" England. And further along on the pages of history we meet up with Sailor's Grog and Buttered Rum, which still number their devotees in large, round figures. (That phrase has two meanings, both of which fit perfectly in this instance.)

But such drinks of other days are few and far between when compared with the palate teasing mixtures of our own liquor-conscious Twentieth Century. For today they are as numerous as the sands of the desert—and far more welcome. There is no end to their names and purposes, no limit to the variety of their ingredients and potentialities.

Some are truly awe-inspiring, so grand in their blending of delicious tastes—and so powerful in their hidden might—that one feels like approaching them on bended knee and with bowed head.

If a brimming bowl of golden Eggnog does not create something closely akin to this feeling in your inner self, then it can only be said that you have missed some of the best things in life. And as for a tall, cool, frosty goblet of the glorious Mint Julep—that epitome of the Southland's hospitality—if you can touch your lips

to its tantalizing rim without a feeling of reverence for that immortal who brewed the first of these wonderful libations to Bacchante, then you must surely be a lost soul.

But these are only the beginnings. What ecstatic dreams, what mouthwatering visions, are "conjured up" by the mere naming of such liquid delights as the Tom and Jerry, the Singapore Sling, the Planter's Punch, and so on and on, ad infinitum.

All these, and countless others, only go to prove the point being made, that the mixing of drinks is an art, and a modern art at that. So with this fact considered as proven, comes now the colossal task of conveying to you some of the secrets of this art's masterpieces. Where to begin, but harder still—where to stop—that is the rub. To slightly misquote:

> "To him who in the love of liquor holds communion with
> her visable forms, she speaks a various language."

To say that it is a various language is putting it very mildly indeed. There are so many kinds of spirits, and so many ways and means of combining them, that the numerical possibilities of their mixture is far beyond the ken of the average mathematical mind. So the problem of listing a representative group of really good drinks, and the recipes for re-creating them, becomes a matter of elimination. Only the outstanding examples of the mixologist's genius—and not even all that deserve such classification—can be given in a modest volume (such as this).

You will find our selections in the following pages. If we have omitted some prime favorites of your convivial moments please pardon the oversight and write them in yourself on one of the blank pages provided for that purpose in the back of the book.

Highballs—The Collins And Rickey
Families—And Some Others

TO even attempt any systematic grouping of the thousands of
mixed drinks that have been, are being, and will be concocted,
is a baffling task. Even the Past Grand Master of the Royal Order
of Barkeepers would confess judgement and pay all costs rather
than make the attempt. Who can pass judicially on whether a Mamie
Taylor is a Highball (it is so called generally) or the girl friend
of Tom Collins? And under what banner is our able friend, the

Gin Buck, supposed to march? Your guess is as good as anyone's.
And so, only a general effort has been made to marshall the
various drinks into clans whose principal characteristics are similar,
mainly with the idea of helping the searcher after new alcoholic
thrills find something that his cellar will enable him to try.

For instance, our first group, which some unkind critics may liken
to Coxey's Army, includes Highballs, Toddies, Skins (honest, that
is what they are called), the popular Collins and Rickey families,
Slings, Sangarees, and a few renegades. Just pay your money and
take your choice of the following.

WHISKEY HIGHBALL
The old reliable.

USE HIGHBALL GLASS, OF COURSE.
HALF FILL WITH CRACKED ICE, ADD
1½ JIGGERS RYE, BOURBON OR
SCOTCH. FILL WITH CARBONATED
WATER, ADD TWIST LEMON PEEL.

GINGER ALE HIGHBALL
Another popular one.

HALF FILL HIGHBALL GLASS WITH
CRACKED ICE, ADD 1½ JIGGERS RYE
OR BOURBON, FILL WITH GINGER ALE.

BRANDY & GINGER ALE

USE HIGHBALL GLASS. PUT IN
2 CUBES ICE, 1 WINEGLASS BRANDY,
FILL WITH GINGER ALE. STIR WITH
SPOON AND SERVE.

BRANDY & SODA
The English love it.

USE HIGHBALL GLASS.
2 CUBES ICE
1 WINEGLASS BRANDY
1 BOTTLE PLAIN SODA
STIR AND SERVE.

GOLF LINKS HIGHBALL

1 TEASPOON PINEAPPLE SYRUP
1 TEASPOON LEMON JUICE
½ WINEGLASS SWEET CATAWBA
½ WINEGLASS RYE WHISKEY
1 DASH MEDFORD RUM
USE HIGHBALL GLASS AND ADD CRACKED
ICE AND CHARGED WATER UNTIL FULL.

ADMIRAL SCHLEY HIGHBALL

1 TEASPOON PINEAPPLE JUICE
1 TEASPOON LEMON JUICE
2/3 WINEGLASS IRISH WHISKEY
PUT IN HIGHBALL GLASS, ADD LUMP
OF ICE AND FILL WITH CARBONATED
WATER.

(Its name dates it.)

UNCLE SAM HIGHBALL
*The Gay Nineties also knew
this one.*

1 TEASPOON LEMON JUICE
1 TEASPOON SYRUP
½ TEASPOON ABRICOTINE
½ WINEGLASS DRY CATAWBA
½ WINEGLASS TOKAY
1 PONY BRANDY
1 SLICE PINEAPPLE
PUT ALL IN HIGHBALL GLASS, ADD
LUMP OF ICE AND CHARGED WATER.

KITTY HIGHBALL

PLACE LUMP OF ICE IN TALL THIN
GLASS. HALF FILL WITH CLARET,
ADD GINGER ALE UNTIL FULL.
STIR AND SERVE.

Bull Dog Highball

Place two cubes ice in
8 oz. highball glass, add juice
of 1 orange and 1 wineglass
Dry Gin. Fill with Ginger Ale.

Mint Highball
Sounds very ladylike.

Place 1 cube ice in 8 oz. highball
glass, add 1 jigger Creme de Menthe.
Fill glass with carbonated water
or Ginger Ale and serve with a
twist of lemon peel.

Morning Glory Highball

1 jigger Brandy
1 jigger Whiskey
3 dashes gum syrup
2 dashes Curacao
2 dashes Bitters
1 dash Absinthe (Pernod)
1 twist lemon peel
Use 8 oz. highball glass, add
2 cubes ice and fill with
seltzer. Just before serving
stir in a little sugar.
(Some highball, we would say!)

Victory Highball

1 jigger Grenadine
1 jigger Anisette
Shake well with cracked ice
and strain into 8 oz. highball
glass, fill with seltzer.
*(Sounds like it was invented for a sorority
celebration.)*

Stone Fence Highball

1 jigger Scotch Whiskey
2 dashes Bitters
Use 8 oz. highball glass,
fill with seltzer after
adding cube of ice.

Sleepy Head Highball

1 jigger Brandy
1 piece orange peel
4 sprigs fresh mint
Add cube of ice and fill
glass with Ginger Ale.
*(Why call it Sleepy Head? Sounds like it
would open your eyes.)*

Whiskey Toddy

1 teaspoon sugar
1/2 glass water
2 jiggers Whiskey
1 small lump of ice
Stir all together in a
toddy glass and serve.

HOT WHISKEY TODDY

1 LUMP SUGAR
DISSOLVE THIS IN A LITTLE
HOT WATER, THEN ADD:
1 PIECE CINNAMON
1 TWIST LEMON PEEL
4 CLOVES
1 JIGGER WHISKEY
FILL TODDY GLASS WITH
HOT WATER AND SERVE.

(Said to be sure death to a cold, but it actually takes several doses—thank heaven!)

OLD KENTUCKY TODDY

USE SILVER GOBLET OR LARGE
TODDY GLASS. FILL 2/3 FULL
OF SMALL LUMPS OF ICE, ADD
DESSERT SPOON OF GRANULATED
SUGAR, DISSOLVED IN LIKE AMOUNT
OF WATER. STIR UNTIL VESSEL
FROSTS, THEN ALMOST FILL WITH
CHOICE WHISKEY AND ADD DESSERT
SPOON OF FINE PEACH BRANDY.
TOP WITH LONG ORANGE PEEL.

(And prepare to dream of the good old days, "befo de war.")

HOT BRICK

1 TEASPOON BUTTER
1 TEASPOON SUGAR
3 PINCHES GROUND CINNAMON
1 JIGGER HOT WATER
MIX THESE IN A SMALL
GOBLET AND THEN ADD:
1 JIGGER FINE WHISKEY
FILL GLASS WITH STEAMING
HOT WATER, SERVE HOT.

(If you are good, they call you a "brick," so both ends of this name express the truth.)

RUM & BUTTER

1 LUMP SUGAR
1 PINCH ALLSPICE
1 PINCH CLOVES
1 JIGGER JAMAICA RUM
DISSOLVE SUGAR IN A LITTLE HOT
WATER, THEN ADD RUM, ALLSPICE
AND CLOVES. FILL GLASS WITH
HOT WATER AND SERVE. DROP
SMALL PIECE OF BUTTER IN THE
GLASS AS YOU SERVE IT.

RHINE WINE & SELTZER
One of the oldest favorites.

USE A LARGE BAR GLASS, FILL
HALF FULL OF RHINE WINE THAT
HAS BEEN THOROUGHLY CHILLED.
THEN FILL GLASS WITH SELTZER,
ALSO RIGHT OFF THE ICE.

(With smierkase and chives and plenty of rye bread, it certainly hits the spot.)

Blue Blazer

USE TWO METAL MUGS. INTO ONE POUR 2 JIGGERS WHISKEY, INTO THE OTHER 2 JIGGERS BOILING WATER. IGNITE THE WHISKEY, AND WHILE BLAZING MIX THE TWO BY POURING FROM ONE MUG TO THE OTHER FIVE OR SIX TIMES. SWEETEN WITH SUGAR AND SERVE WITH A TWIST OF

(Jerry Thomas, most famous of bartenders, invented this drink, and he was expert enough to mix it succesfully. Amateurs would be well advised to have a fire extinguisher handy.)

Black Stripe

USE SMALL BAR GLASS.
1 WINEGLASS SANTA CRUZ
    OR JAMAICA RUM
1 TABLESPOON MOLASSES
1 TABLESPOON WATER
FILL GLASS WITH SHAVED ICE
AND STIR THOROUGHLY.

Bon Soir

USE SHERRY GLASS.
½ PONY CREME YVETTE
½ PONY BENEDICTINE
HALF FILL GLASS WITH ICE,
ADD GINGER 'LE TILL GLASS
IS BRIMMING FULL. STIR GENTLY
AND SERVE WITH A STRAW.

(It means "Good Evening." Why not?)

Mulled Claret

USING SMALL PAN, MIX THESE
INGREDIENTS:
3 LUMPS SUGAR
2 DASHES LEMON JUICE
4 WHOLE ALLSPICE (BRUISED)
2 WHOLE CLOVES (BRUISED)
1/3 TEASPOON GROUND CINNAMON
2 WINEGLASSES CLARET
LET COMPOUND BOIL FOR TWO
MINUTES, STIRRING CONTINUOUSLY,
THEN STRAIN INTO LARGE BAR GLASS.

Applejack Algonquin

1 TEASPOON BAKED APPLE
1 LUMP SUGAR
1 JIGGER APPLEJACK
FILL GLASS WITH HOT WATER.

(Perhaps this is just applesauce.)

GIVE STRONG DRINK UNTO HIM THAT IS ABOUT TO PERIS
AND WINE UNTO THOSE THAT BE OF HEAVY HEART.
LET HIM DRINK AND FORGET HIS POVERTY, AND REMEMBE
HIS MISERY NO MORE.

CUBA LIBRE

1/4 OUNCE LIME JUICE
1 JIGGER FINE RUM
PUT THESE IN HIGHBALL GLASS
FULL OF CRACKED ICE, THEN ADD
COCA-COLA UNTIL GLASS IS
BRIMMING FULL. STIR WELL.

(Here's the coke addict's only chance.)

BRANDY SKIN

USE WHISKEY GLASS.
1/2 GLASS HOT WATER
1 JIGGER BRANDY
STIR AND SERVE WITH TWIST
OF LEMON PEEL. (THE LAST IS
THE TOUCH THAT GIVES THE
DRINK ITS NAME. DON'T
FORGET IT.)

GIN SKIN

MADE AND SERVED SAME AS BRANDY
SKIN, USING GIN INSTEAD OF
BRANDY.

WHISKEY SKIN

MADE AND SERVED SAME AS BRANDY
SKIN, USING WHISKEY INSTEAD
OF BRANDY.

SHANDY GAFF
One of the old timers.

1/2 GLASS BEER
1/2 GLASS GINGER ALE

(The name isn't the only funny thing about it.)

HORSE'S NECK
With a kick.

USE 8 OZ. TUMBLER.
PEEL LEMON SO RIND IS IN ONE
LONG SPIRAL PIECE AND PLACE
IN GLASS WITH ONE END HANGING
OVER THE RIM. FILL GLASS WITH
ICE CUBES, ADD 1 JIGGER WHISKEY
AND FILL WITH GINGER ALE. STIR.

(Leave out the whiskey and you leave out the kick. The original Horse's Neck had no kick, so one might suspect that as the reason for the name. Certainly the neck is the wrong end for kicking. But in reality, the name comes from the shape the lemon spiral takes when hung over the rim of the glass.)

GIN BUCK

JUICE OF 1/2 LEMON
1 JIGGER DRY GIN
USE 8 OZ. HIGHBALL GLASS, ADD
CUBE OF ICE, FILL WITH GINGER
ALE AND STIR WELL.

(After two or three of these, you can "buck" as hard as any broncho.)

MAMIE TAYLOR

USE HIGHBALL GLASS.
1 JIGGER WHISKEY
½ LIME (JUICE ONLY)
ADD SOME CRACKED ICE
AND FILL WITH GINGER ALE.
*(Nobody seems to know who Mamie Taylor
was, but her name will never die.)*

TOM COLLINS
*Made originally with Old Tom
Gin, hence the name.*

JUICE OF 1 LIME
  (OR ½ LEMON)
1 TEASPOON POWDERED SUGAR
1 JIGGER DRY GIN
USE TALL GLASS. ADD CUBE
OF ICE AND CARBONATED WATER, STIR.

JOHN COLLINS
Really the oldest.

MADE SAME AS TOM COLLINS,
USING HOLLAND GIN INSTEAD OF DRY.

TOM COLLINS WHISKEY

1 SMALL LEMON (JUICE ONLY)
5 DASHES SYRUP
2 JIGGERS WHISKEY
PUT INGREDIENTS IN A TALL GLASS,
ADD CUBE OF ICE AND CARBONATED
WATER, THEN STIR.

RUM COLLINS

1 LEMON (JUICE ONLY)
1 TEASPOON POWDERED SUGAR
1 JIGGER RUM
USE TOM COLLINS GLASS, ADD
ICE AND FILL WITH SELTZER
WATER. STIR WELL AND TOP
WITH SLICE OF LEMON.
(He's a rum sort of cove.)

SANDY COLLINS

1 JIGGER SCOTCH WHISKEY
1 TEASPOON POWDERED SUGAR
½ LEMON (JUICE ONLY)
PUT SEVERAL CUBES OF ICE IN
TOM COLLINS GLASS, ADD ABOVE.
FILL WITH SELTZER AND STIR.

THOMAS & JEREMIAH

USE TALL GLASS.
1½ JIGGERS WHITE RUM
2 DASHES LIME JUICE
ADD BROWN SUGAR TO TASTE
(BE SURE IT'S BROWN), AND
FILL GLASS WITH HOT SWEET CIDER.
(—and pleasant dreams perhaps.)

GIN RICKEY

½ LIME
1 JIGGER DRY GIN
HALF FILL GLASS WITH ICE,
SQUEEZE LIME OVER SAME, ADD
RIND AND GIN, FILL WITH
CARBONATED WATER AND STIR.

(This was named after a well known character of another day, Col. Joe Rickey, of Washington, DC.)

WHISKEY RICKEY

MADE SAME AS GIN RICKEY,
SUBSTITUTING RYE OR BOURBON
FOR THE GIN.

SLOE GIN RICKEY

MADE SAME AS REGULAR GIN
RICKEY, USING SLOE GIN
INSTEAD OF DRY GIN.

(And it isn't so slow!)

GIN SLING
Sounds Chinese, but isn't.

1 TEASPOON SUGAR, DISSOLVED
IN WATER, USING HIGHBALL GLASS.
ADD CUBE OF ICE AND 1 JIGGER
DRY GIN. STIR AND FILL GLASS
WITH EITHER PLAIN OR CARBONATED
WATER.

WHISKEY SLING

MADE THE SAME AS A GIN SLING,
SUBSTITUTING FINE WHISKEY
FOR THE GIN.

HOT SCOTCH SLING

1 JIGGER SCOTCH WHISKEY
1 LUMP SUGAR
DISSOLVE THE SUGAR IN HIGHBALL
GLASS 3/4 FULL OF BOILING WATER.
ADD WHISKEY AND GRATE NUTMEG ON
TOP.

(Might be called Hop Scotch—it will make you jump.)

SINGAPORE SLING
The real article.

1 JIGGER SLOE GIN
1/2 JIGGER DRY GIN
1/2 JIGGER APRICOT BRANDY
1/2 JIGGER CHERRY BRANDY
1/2 LIME (JUICE ONLY)
1 TEASPOON SUGAR
MIX THESE IN 12 OZ. GLASS,
ADD ICE AND FILL WITH SELTZER.
DECORATE WITH CHERRY, SLICE OF
ORANGE, AND PIECE OF PINEAPPLE
COLORED RED.

(And how you can sling them down the hatch is nobody's business.)

SINGAPORE SLING

This one was censored.

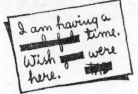

JUICE OF 1/2 LIME
1/2 JIGGER DRY GIN
1 JIGGER CHERRY BRANDY
1 DASH BENEDICTINE
SHAKE WELL WITH ICE, SERVE IN
TOM COLLINS GLASS AND FILL WITH
SELTZER WATER. DECORATE WITH
FRUIT.

STRAITS SLING

1 JIGGER DRY GIN
JUICE OF 1/2 LEMON
3 DASHES BENEDICTINE
3 DASHES CHERRY BRANDY
1 DASH BITTERS
SHAKE WELL WITH ICE, SERVE IN
TOM COLLINS GLASS, FILLING IT
WITH SELTZER WATER. DECORATE
WITH FRUIT.

BRANDY SANGAREE

1 JIGGER BRANDY
1 PONY WATER
1 TEASPOON POWDERED SUGAR
STIR THESE IN A 4 OZ. GLASS
ABOUT $\frac{1}{4}$ FULL OF SHAVED ICE,
ADD A DASH OF PORT WINE AND SERVE.

(Can't tell you why the port is there.)

GIN SANGAREE

1 TEASPOON POWDERED SUGAR
1 JIGGER HOLLAND GIN
DISSOLVE SUGAR IN A LITTLE
WATER, STIR SUGAR AND GIN IN
4 OZ. GLASS ABOUT $\frac{1}{4}$ FULL OF
SHAVED ICE, ADD TEASPOON SHERRY
ON TOP.

PORT SANGAREE

USE LARGE BAR GLASS, HALF FILL
WITH FINE ICE. ADD 1 TEASPOON
POWDERED SUGAR AND $1\frac{1}{2}$ WINEGLASSES
PORT WINE. SHAKE WELL, STRAIN INTO
FANCY STEM GLASS AND SERVE WITH
NUTMEG ON TOP.

SHERRY SANGAREE

MAKE THE SAME AS PORT SANGAREE,
USING SHERRY IN PLACE OF PORT.

FILL EVERY BEAKER UP, MY MEN, POUR FORTH
    THE CHEERING WINE:
THERE'S LIFE AND STRENGTH IN EVERY DROP,
    - THANKSGIVING TO THE VINE!
      —FROM "THE BARON'S LAST BANQUET".

Some "Well Dressed" Drinks

T HE "four hundred" of the mixed drink world, the "real Bon Tons," might be said to include the Juleps and the Punches (the singles, or bachelors). They are classed as the elite of spiritual society because they are the swellest dressers. Whenever they appear at parties they are invariably all "dolled up" in bright colors and trimmed in the fresh fruits of the season. And do they hand out the icy stares? They fairly freeze you!

The head of the house is Colonel Mint Julep, a southerner of the old school, and his retainers, (besides the bachelor Punches, so designated to keep you from confusing them with the more plebian Punch families), include the Sours, Cobblers, Daisies, Crustas, Fixes, Coolers and Smashes.

Colonel Mint Julep has come close to causing another war in the south. Kentucky, Georgia, and Maryland each have their special way of introducing him to society, and each insists that the other's method constitutes a sacrilege. "To bruise or not to bruise" the mint, "that is the question." We have played safe by listing all three states' ways of celebrating the rites.

The Planter's Punch has also caused punches to fly on many occasions. Some devotees add enough fruit and spinach to suggest Saturday night at the market, while the dyed-in-the-wool Planter's Punchers—or is it Punch Planters—say that such treatment of this patriarch of the Caribbeans is a crime. Again we stick strictly to a non-belligerent policy, and give you several treatments to choose from.

KENTUCKY MINT JULEP

PUT 12 SPRIGS FRESH MINT IN BOWL, COVER WITH POWDERED SUGAR AND JUST ENOUGH WATER TO DISSOLVE SUGAR. CRUSH WITH WOODEN PESTLE. PLACE HALF THE CRUSHED MINT AND LIQUID IN BOTTOM OF A 12 OZ. TUMBLER, HALF FILL WITH CRUSHED ICE, ADD REST OF MINT LIQUID AND FINISH FILLING GLASS WITH ICE. POUR IN BOURBON WHISKEY UNTIL GLASS IS BRIMMING FULL, AND PLACE IN REFRIGERATOR FOR AN HOUR OR SO (GET THEE BEHIND ME, SATAN). SERVE WITH MINT LEAVES DIPPED IN POWDERED SUGAR.

GEORGIA MINT JULEP

4 SPRIGS FRESH MINT
½ TABLESPOON POWDERED SUGAR
1½ JIGGERS FINE WHISKEY
PLACE ALL IN LARGE GLASS, FILL WITH CRUSHED ICE AND STIR GENTLY UNTIL GLASS IS FROSTED. DECORATE WITH MINT LEAVES. (NOTE THAT THE MINT IS NOT BRUISED IN THIS RECIPE.)

MARYLAND MINT JULEP

1½ TEASPOONS POWDERED SUGAR
    DISSOLVE THIS IN WATER.
4 SPRIGS FRESH MINT
    BRUISE, BUT DO NOT CRUSH.
2 JIGGERS RYE WHISKEY
PUT THESE IN A TALL GLASS FILLED WITH CRUSHED ICE, STIR UNTIL FROSTED AND DECORATE WITH SOME MORE MINT.

(This might be called the "Maryland Compromise.")

BRANDY JULEP

USE LARGE GOBLET, FILL WITH FINE ICE AND ADD 1 JIGGER COGNAC. MUDDLE SEVERAL SPRIGS OF FRESH MINT IN A LITTLE WATER AND SUGAR, STRAIN THIS LIQUID INTO THE GOBLET. ADD 1 DASH JAMAICA RUM, STIR AND DRESS WITH FRUIT AND FEW SPRIGS OF MINT DIPPED IN SUGAR. SERVE WITH A STRAW.

"GIVE AN IRISHMAN LAGER FOR A MONTH AND HE'S A DEAD MAN. AN IRISHMAN IS LINED WITH COPPER AND THE BEER CORRODES IT. BUT WHISKEY POLISHES THE COPPER AND IS THE SAVING OF HIM."
— MARK TWAIN

MAJOR BAILEY
OR GIN JULEP

USE TOM COLLINS GLASS.
4 SPRIGS FRESH MINT
    ENOUGH POWDERED SUGAR
    TO COVER.
½ LEMON (JUICE ONLY)
CRUSH MINT WITH MUDDLER, ADD
1½ JIGGERS DRY GIN AND FILL
GLASS WITH CRUSHED ICE. STIR
UNTIL GLASS IS FROSTED, THEN
DECORATE WITH MINT SPRIGS AND
SERVE WITH A STRAW.

(Another Kentucky invention, we presume, though we didn't know why they had any mere majors in Kentucky.)

CHAMPAGNE JULEP

USE MEDIUM SIZE THIN GLASS,
HALF FILLED WITH SHAVED ICE.
ADD 1 LUMP SUGAR AND
2 SPRIGS FRESH MINT. POUR
CHAMPAGNE IN SLOWLY UNTIL
FULL AND STIR GENTLY. DECORATE
WITH FRUIT, ADD A DASH OF
BRANDY, AND SERVE WITH A STRAW.

(Fit for a king they say, but you don't have to be a king to enjoy it. Who wants to be a king these days, anyway?)

BISHOP
Ought to be good.

USE LARGE BAR GLASS.
1 TEASPOON POWDERED SUGAR
2 DASHES LEMON JUICE
2 TWISTS LEMON PEEL
1 DASH CARBONATED WATER
2 DASHES JAMAICA RUM
3/4 GLASS SHAVED ICE
FILL GLASS WITH CLARET OR
BURGUNDY, SHAKE WELL, DEC-
ORATE WITH FRUIT AND SERVE
WITH A STRAW.

FIELD CLUB
SPECIAL

1 LIME (JUICE ONLY)
2 DASHES GRENADINE
2 JIGGERS RUM
3 SPRIGS FRESH MINT (CRUSHED)
SERVE IN TALL 14 OZ. GLASS
FILLED WITH SHAVED ICE. STIR
UNTIL FROSTED, DECORATE WITH
A CHERRY AND SPRIG OF MINT,
TOP WITH A DASH OF RHUM NEGRITA.

ABSINTHE FRAPPE

USE MIXING GLASS AND
FILL WITH SHAVED ICE.
1 TEASPOON BENEDICTINE
1 PONY ABSINTHE (PERNOD)
1 WINEGLASS WATER
SHAKE UNTIL OUTSIDE OF GLASS
IS FROSTED, THEN STRAIN INTO
6 OZ. GLASS.

BRANDY SHAKE

1 JIGGER COGNAC
1 TABLESPOON SUGAR
2 LIMES (JUICE ONLY)
SHAKE THESE WELL IN SMALL
MIXING GLASS, ALMOST FULL
OF FINE ICE. STRAIN INTO
FANCY STEM GLASS AND SERVE.
(THIS DRINK CAN ALSO BE MADE
WITH GIN, WHISKEY OR RUM.)

WHISKEY SOUR

½ LEMON (JUICE ONLY)
½ TEASPOON POWDERED SUGAR
1 JIGGER WHISKEY
ADD CRACKED ICE AND SHAKE WELL,
STRAIN INTO A DELMONICO GLASS
AND FILL WITH CARBONATED WATER.

*(A pick-me-up that has no equal. Too many
will do just as well to lay you out.)*

BRANDY SOUR

MADE AND SERVED SAME AS
WHISKEY SOUR, USING BRANDY
INSTEAD OF WHISKEY.

APPLEJACK SOUR

1 TEASPOON SYRUP
2 TEASPOONS PINEAPPLE SYRUP
1 TEASPOON LEMON JUICE
1 WINEGLASS APPLEJACK
STIR THESE IN A MIXING GLASS
HALF FULL OF SHAVED ICE, THEN
STRAIN INTO A DELMONICO GLASS.
FILL WITH CARBONATED WATER AND
DRESS WITH FRUIT.

JAMAICA RUM SOUR

½ LEMON (JUICE ONLY)
½ LIME (JUICE ONLY)
1 PONY GUM SYRUP
1 JIGGER JAMAICA RUM
MIX AND SERVE THE SAME
AS OTHER SOURS.

EGG SOUR

1 TEASPOON POWDERED SUGAR
3 DASHES LEMON JUICE
1 DASH CURACAO
1 JIGGER BRANDY
1 EGG
SHAKE WELL IN MIXING GLASS,
HALF FULL OF SHAVED ICE.
STRAIN INTO DELMONICO GLASS.

GIN SOUR

1 TEASPOON SUGAR
4 DASHES LEMON OR LIME JUICE
1 WINEGLASS HOLLAND GIN
MIX AND SERVE SAME AS
OTHER SOURS.

SCARLETT O'HARA
Yes, it's new.

1 JIGGER BOURBON
1 LIME (JUICE ONLY)
1/4 PEACH (CANNED, COLORED RED)
PLACE THESE IN YOUR ELECTRIC
MIXER AND ADD QUANTITY OF
SHAVED ICE. BLEND UNTIL
THOROUGHLY FRAPPED, SERVE IN
SAUCER CHAMPAGNE GLASS.

(Supposed to be especially for the ladies—
but you know how the men felt about Scarlett!)

RHETT BUTTLER
And so is this.

1 TEASPOON CURACAO
1 JIGGER WHISKEY
1/2 LIME (JUICE ONLY)
1/3 LEMON (JUICE ONLY)
1/2 TEASPOON SUGAR
PLACE IN ELECTRIC MIXER WITH
SHAVED ICE, BLEND THOROUGHLY
AND SERVE IN SAUCER CHAMPAGNE
GLASS.

(And this was concocted for men—
but Rhett has some lady friends, too!)

MARY PICKFORD
An older vintage.

2 BARSPOONS GRENADINE
4 STICKS OF FRESH PINEAPPLE
MUDDLE THESE AND ADD;
1 JIGGER FINE RUM
3 TABLESPOONS SHAVED ICE
PLACE ABOVE IN ELECTRIC MIXER,
BLEND THOROUGHLY, THEN STRAIN
INTO SAUCER CHAMPAGNE GLASS.

(America's Sweetheart—in a new make-up.)

WHISKEY COBBLER
No. 1

1 TEASPOON POWDERED SUGAR
1 JIGGER WHISKEY
STIR THESE IN A HIGHBALL GLASS
HALF FILLED WITH CRACKED ICE.
DECORATE WITH SLICES OF
ORANGE AND PINEAPPLE.

WHISKEY COBBLER
No. 2
We vote for this one.

1 JIGGER WHISKEY
1/2 PONY CURACAO
1/2 LEMON (JUICE ONLY)
1 SLICE LEMON
1 SLICE ORANGE
STIR LIQUID INGREDIENTS WITH
ICE IN HIGHBALL GLASS UNTIL IT
IS FROSTED, THEN ADD FRUIT.

BRANDY COBBLER

DISSOLVE 1 TEASPOON POWDERED
SUGAR IN A LITTLE WATER IN A
LARGE BAR GLASS. ADD 1 WINEGLASS
BRANDY AND FILL WITH CRACKED ICE.
SHAKE WELL, ORNAMENT WITH FRUIT,
SERVE WITH STRAWS.

SHERRY COBBLER

2 JIGGERS IMPORTED SHERRY
1 TEASPOON POWDERED SUGAR
1 TWISTED LEMON PEEL
HALF FILL A HIGHBALL GLASS WITH
SHAVED ICE, ADD THE ABOVE AND
STIR UNTIL GLASS IS FROSTED.
GARNISH WITH ORANGE AND PINEAPPLE

CHAMPAGNE COBBLER
The head of the class.

USE LARGE BAR GLASS.
1 TEASPOON SUGAR
1 SLICE ORANGE PEEL
1 SLICE LEMON PEEL
1/2 GLASS SHAVED ICE
ADD CHAMPAGNE TO FILL GLASS,
DECORATE WITH FRUITS AND
BERRIES. SERVE WITH STRAW.

PORT COBBLER

2 TABLESPOONS POWDERED SUGAR
$1\frac{1}{2}$ WINEGLASS PORT WINE
1 JIGGER MINERAL WATER
STIR THE ABOVE INTO HIGHBALL
GLASS HALF FILLED WITH CRACKED
ICE. WHEN GLASS IS FROSTED
DRESS WITH FRUIT AND SERVE
WITH STRAW.

CALIFORNIA SHERRY COBBLER

1 PONY PINEAPPLE SYRUP
2 WINEGLASSES CALIFORNIA SHERRY
SHAKE THE ABOVE IN A LARGE BAR
GLASS WITH CRACKED ICE, DRESS
WITH FRUIT, THEN GENTLY FLOAT
A LITTLE PORT WINE ON TOP.

("California, here we come!")

RUM COBBLER

1 TEASPOON POWDERED SUGAR
2 DASHES CARBONATED WATER
1 JIGGER RUM
USING TOM COLLINS GLASS, STIR
THE ABOVE WITH PLENTY OF SHAVED
ICE, GARNISH WITH FRUIT, AND
SERVE WITH A STRAW.

SAUTERNE COBBLER

2 JIGGERS SAUTERNE
1/2 JIGGER ORCHARD SYRUP
POUR THESE INTO A LARGE BAR
GLASS, FILL WITH CRACKED ICE
AND STIR WELL. DRESS WITH FRUIT
AND SERVE WITH A STRAW.

GIN COBBLER

MADE IN THE SAME WAY AS THE
RUM COBBLER, SUBSTITUTING
DRY GIN FOR THE RUM.

CLARET COBBLER

USE LARGE BAR GLASS.
1 TEASPOON SUGAR, DISSOLVED
    IN A LITTLE WATER.
2 WINEGLASSES CLARET
FILL GLASS WITH FINE ICE, STIR
WELL AND DECORATE WITH SLICE
OF ORANGE, QUARTERED.

WHISKEY DAISY
No-1
All its name implies.

1/2 LIME (JUICE ONLY)
1/4 LEMON (JUICE ONLY)
2 DASHES GRENADINE
2 DASHES CARBONATED WATER
1 JIGGER WHISKEY
PUT THESE INGREDIENTS IN A
HIGHBALL GLASS, FILL WITH
CRUSHED ICE, STIR UNTIL GLASS
IS FROSTED. DECORATE WITH
FRUIT AND FRESH MINT AND
SERVE WITH A STRAW.

HERE'S TO THE MAN IN THE MOON!
THE FULLER HE GETS THE BRIGHTER HE GROWS.

GIN DAISY

MADE SAME AS A WHISKEY DAISY EXCEPT THAT YOU SUBSTITUTE DRY GIN FOR THE WHISKEY. (BRANDY OR RUM MAY ALSO BE SUBSTITUTED IF DESIRED.)

BRANDY DAISY

4 DASHES GUM SYRUP
3 DASHES CURACAO
1/2 LEMON (JUICE ONLY)
3 DASHES ORANGE CORDIAL
1 WINEGLASS BRANDY
SHAKE WELL WITH CRACKED ICE AND ADD CARBONATED WATER TO SUIT. SERVE IN SMALL BAR GLASS. (GIN AND RUM DAISIES MAY ALSO BE MADE THIS WAY.)

CANADIAN DAISY

1/2 LEMON (JUICE ONLY)
1 JIGGER WHISKEY
1 PONY RASPBERRY SYRUP
SHAKE WELL WITH CRACKED ICE AND SERVE IN 8 OZ. GLASS, ADDING SODA WATER TO SUIT. TRIM WITH FRUIT.

WHISKEY DAISY
No. 2

1/2 TABLESPOON SUGAR
4 DASHES LEMON JUICE
1 DASH LIME JUICE
1 PONY CARBONATED WATER
1 JIGGER WHISKEY
1/2 PONY CHARTREUSE
PREPARE AND SERVE THE SAME AS OTHER DAISIES.

LAUDER'S DAISY
The one he sings about.

1 JIGGER SCOTCH WHISKEY
1 PONY SIMPLE SYRUP
JUICE OF 1/2 LEMON AND 1/2 LIME. PREPARE AND SERVE THE SAME AS OTHER DAISIES.
(Bet you were surprised at the kind of whiskey used.)

SANTA CRUZ DAISY

3 DASHES GUM SYRUP
3 DASHES CURACAO
JUICE OF 1/2 LEMON
1 JIGGER SANTA CRUZ RUM
PREPARE AND SERVE AS OTHER DAISIES.

BRANDY CRUSTA
Better practice on this.

4 DASHES GUM SYRUP
2 DASHES ANGOSTURA BITTERS
2 DASHES LEMON JUICE
2 DASHES MARASCHINO
1 JIGGER BRANDY
NOW TAKE A BRIGHT COLORED
LEMON ABOUT THE SIZE OF YOUR
WINE GLASS AND PEEL THE RIND
IN ONE PIECE. MOISTEN THE RIM
OF THE GLASS WITH LEMON AND
DIP IT INTO POWDERED SUGAR TO
GIVE A FROSTED EFFECT, THEN
FIT THE LEMON PEEL INSIDE THE
GLASS. AFTER SHAKING THE
INGREDIENTS WITH CRACKED ICE,
STRAIN INTO THIS GLASS.

GIN CRUSTA

MADE AND SERVED THE SAME AS
BRANDY CRUSTA, SUBSTITUTING
GIN FOR BRANDY.

ST. CROIX CRUSTA

4 DASHES ORCHARD SYRUP
1 DASH ANGOSTURA BITTERS
1 DASH LEMON JUICE
2 DASHES MARASCHINO
1 JIGGER ST. CROIX RUM
PREPARE AND SERVE IN SPECIAL
GLASS, SAME AS BRANDY CRUSTA.

WHISKEY CRUSTA

4 DASHES GUM SYRUP
2 DASHES ANGOSTURA BITTERS
2 DASHES LEMON JUICE
2 DASHES CURACAO
1 JIGGER WHISKEY
PREPARE AND SERVE IN SPECIAL
GLASS, SAME AS BRANDY CRUSTA.

GIN FIX
How expressive a name.

1 HEAPING TEASPOON POWDERED
  SUGAR
1/2 LEMON (JUICE ONLY
1 JIGGER WATER
2 JIGGERS DRY GIN
TO A HIGHBALL GLASS 2/3 FULL
OF SHAVED ICE, ADD THE ABOVE
INGREDIENTS. STIR THOROUGHLY
AND DECORATE WITH FRUIT.

WHISKEY FIX

MADE IN THE SAME WAY AS THE
GIN FIX, USING WHISKEY INSTEAD
OF GIN.

APPLEJACK FIX

USE LARGE BAR GLASS, FILL WITH
ICE AND ADD THE FOLLOWING:
1 TEASPOON SUGAR
1/2 LEMON (JUICE ONLY)
2 DASHES CURACAO
1/2 PONY FRUIT SYRUP
1 WINEGLASS APPLEJACK
STIR WELL, DECORATE WITH ORANGE
AND PINEAPPLE, SERVE WITH A STRAW.

(May get you in a fix, if you're not careful.)

BRANDY FIX

MADE IN THE SAME WAY AS APPLEJACK
FIX, USING BRANDY INSTEAD OF
APPLEJACK.

SANTA CRUZ RUM FIX

1 TEASPOON POWDERED SUGAR
1 PONY WATER
3 DASHES LEMON JUICE
1/2 PONY FRUIT SYRUP
1 JIGGER SANTA CRUZ RUM
STIR WELL IN BAR GLASS FILLED
WITH ICE, THEN DECORATE WITH FRUIT.

BACARDI PEACH

USE A TALL GLASS. DISSOLVE
1 TEASPOON SUGAR IN A LITTLE
WATER, CRUSH 4 MINT LEAVES, ADD
JUICE OF 2 LEMONS, THEN 3 JIGGERS
BACARDI RUM. NOW A LAYER OF
SHAVED ICE, AND 1 WHOLE PITTED
PEACH. AGAIN A LAYER OF ICE,
DRESS WITH MINT LEAVES AND
SERVE WITH A STRAW.

(If you can't drink it you might use it to trim a window.)

KNICKERBOCKER

3 TEASPOONS RASPBERRY SYRUP
1/2 LEMON (JUICE ONLY)
1 WINEGLASS ST. CROIX RUM
1/2 WINEGLASS CURACAO
FILL LARGE BAR GLASS WITH SHAVED
ICE AND ADD THE ABOVE. STIR WELL
AND DRESS WITH SLICES OF ORANGE
AND PINEAPPLE. SERVE WITH STRAW.

HERE'S TO YOUR GOOD HELT,
UND YOUR FAMILY'S GOOD HELT,
UND MAY YOU ALL LIVE LONG UND BROSPER!
— RIP VAN WINKLE ?

MORNING CALL

1/2 JIGGER LIME OR LEMON JUICE
1/2 JIGGER MARASCHINO
1/2 JIGGER ABSINTHE (PERNOD)
STIR THESE IN A LARGE BAR GLASS
HALF FULL OF SHAVED ICE, DRESS
WITH FRUIT AND SERVE WITH STRAW.

BOSTON COOLER

1/2 LEMON (JUICE ONLY)
1/4 TEASPOON POWDERED SUGAR
1 JIGGER RUM
STIR THESE IN A TOM COLLINS
GLASS, FILL WITH CRACKED ICE
AND CARBONATED WATER.

REMSEN COOLER
From the Gay Nineties.

PEEL RIND OF LEMON IN SPIRAL
FORM AND PLACE IN 10 OZ. GLASS.
ADD 3 LUMPS OF ICE AND
1 JIGGER OLD TOM GIN.
FILL GLASS WITH SODA WATER.

HIGHLAND COOLER

1 TEASPOON POWDERED SUGAR
1/2 LEMON (JUICE ONLY)
2 DASHES BITTERS
1 JIGGER SCOTCH WHISKEY
1 LUMP OF ICE
USE 10 OUNCE TUMBLER, FILL
WITH GINGER ALE.

MANHATTAN COOLER

1/2 LIME (JUICE ONLY)
1/2 TABLESPOON POWDERED SUGAR
1½ JIGGERS CLARET
3 DASHES RUM
2 LUMPS ICE
STIR WELL AND STRAIN INTO 7 OZ.
GLASS. FILL WITH CARBONATED
WATER.

(This gets our vote in its class.)

TROPIC COOLER

1 JIGGER WHISKEY
1/2 LIME (JUICE ONLY)
2 CUBES OF ICE
PUT THESE IN TALL HIGHBALL
GLASS AND FILL WITH PLAIN
SODA.

HERE IS A RIDDLE MOST ABSTRUSE,
CANST READ THE ANSWER RIGHT?
WHY IS IT THAT MY TONGUE GROWS LOOSE,
ONLY WHEN I GROW TIGHT?

WHISKEY SMASH
Another expressive name.

USE OLD FASHIONED COCKTAIL GLASS. DISSOLVE 1 LUMP OF SUGAR IN A FEW DASHES OF CARBONATED WATER, ADD FOUR SPRIGS FRESH MINT AND CRUSH SLIGHTLY. FILL GLASS WITH CRACKED ICE, ADD 1 JIGGER OF RYE OR BOURBON, DECORATE WITH LEMON PEEL AND SLICE OF ORANGE.

GIN SMASH

MADE AS WHISKEY SMASH, EXCEPT THAT DRY GIN IS USED INSTEAD OF WHISKEY.

PLANTER'S PUNCH (1)
As made by a West Indian, for a West Indian.

MIX 1 PONY LIME JUICE WITH TWICE AS MUCH SUGAR, THEN ADD 2 JIGGERS OLD JAMAICA RUM AND THE SAME AMOUNT OF WATER AND ICE. SHAKE AND SERVE VERY COLD. (NOTE THAT THERE IS NO FRUIT TRIMMING.)

PLANTER'S PUNCH (2)
As concocted for the American tourist.

1 TEASPOON POWDERED SUGAR
2 TEASPOONS LIME JUICE
2 JIGGERS OLD JAMAICA RUM
STIR THESE IN TALL GLASS FILLED WITH ICE, THEN ADD 1/2 SLICE EACH OF LEMON AND ORANGE, A PIECE OF PINEAPPLE, A CHERRY AND A SPRIG OF MINT.

(They say the garbage man does a good business where this is served.)

PLANTER'S PUNCH (3)
As mixed by "Sandy" of the Chatham Bar, Montejo Bay, Jamaica.

2 JIGGERS JAMAICA RUM
1 JIGGER LIME JUICE
1/2 JIGGER SYRUP
SHAKE WELL, POUR INTO TALL GLASS FILLED WITH ICE, DECORATE WITH FRUIT.

"No. 21" PUNCH

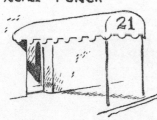

1½ LIMES (JUICE ONLY)
1/4 ORANGE (JUICE ONLY)
1 JIGGER WHISKEY
3/4 TEASPOON POWDERED SUGAR
SHAKE WELL, STRAIN INTO TALL GLASS FILLED WITH CRACKED ICE, DECORATE WITH FRUIT AND FLOAT A LITTLE CLARET ON TOP.

SIR CHARLES PUNCH
An English holiday special.

HALF FILL LARGE TUMBLER WITH
SHAVED ICE, THEN ADD:
1 TEASPOON GRANULATED SUGAR
1 WINEGLASS PORT
1/2 WINEGLASS BRANDY
1/2 WINEGLASS CURACAO
STIR WELL WITH A SPOON,
ORNAMENT TOP WITH SLICES OF
ORANGE, PINEAPPLE AND
SPLIT GRAPES.

SOYER AU CHAMPAGNE
*A Christmas favorite on
the continent.*

PUT TWO LARGE TABLESPOONS
VANILLA ICE CREAM IN A LARGE
TUMBLER, THEN ADD:
2 DASHES MARASCHINO
2 DASHES CURACAO
2 DASHES BRANDY
FILL GLASS TO TOP WITH
CHAMPAGNE AND STIR WELL.
BEFORE SERVING DECORATE WITH
SLICES OF PINEAPPLE, ORANGE
AND LEMON, ALSO CHERRIES
AND BERRIES.

MISSISSIPPI PUNCH
From the deep south, suh.

2 TEASPOONS POWDERED SUGAR
1 PONY WATER
3 DASHES LEMON JUICE
1/2 PONY BOURBON
1/2 PONY JAMAICA RUM
1/2 PONY BRANDY
FILL GOBLET WITH SHAVED ICE,
STIR IN THE ABOVE AND DRESS
WITH ORANGE AND PINEAPPLE.

MILLIONAIRE PUNCH

1 LEMON (JUICE ONLY)
1 DASH LIME JUICE
1 TEASPOON SUGAR
1 JIGGER BOURBON
2 DASHES GRENADINE
SHAKE WELL WITH CRACKED ICE,
STRAIN INTO A GOBLET, ADD A
DASH OF CREME DE MENTHE, AND
DRESS WITH FRUIT.

*(Another reason for wanting to be a
bloated plutocrat.)*

HERE'S TO THE MAIDEN OF BASHFUL FIFTEEN;
    HERE'S TO THE WIDOW OF FIFTY;
HERE'S TO THE FLAUNTING, EXTRAVAGANT QUEEN,
    AND HERE'S TO THE HOUSEWIFE THAT'S THRIFTY!
        LET THE TOAST PASS;
        DRINK TO THE LASS;
I'LL WARRANT SHE'LL PROVE AN EXCUSE FOR THE GLASS!
        — FROM "THE SCHOOL FOR SCANDAL".

PLYMOUTH PUNCH

MUDDLE 1/4 LEMON PEEL AND 1/2 TABLESPOON SUGAR IN A GLASS, ADD 1/3 JIGGER SLOE GIN AND 2/3 JIGGER RYE WHISKEY. STIR WELL AND STRAIN INTO AN OLD STYLE CHAMPAGNE GLASS CONTAINING 1/2 FRESH PEACH. ADD 2 DASHES MEDFORD RUM ON TOP.

(May have been called Plymouth because it will rock you to sleep.)

CHOCOLATE PUNCH

1 TEASPOON SUGAR
1 WINEGLASS PORT WINE
1 PONY CURACAO
1 WHOLE EGG
PUT THESE IN BAR GLASS HALF FULL OF FINE ICE, ADD MILK TILL FULL, SHAKE WELL AND STRAIN INTO PUNCH GLASS. SPRINKLE WITH NUTMEG AND SERVE.
(THE PORT CAUSES THE MILK TO TURN CHOCOLATE BROWN. HENCE THE NAME.)

SOLAR PLEXUS PUNCH

1 TABLESPOON SUGAR
1 TABLESPOON PINEAPPLE SYRUP
1/2 LEMON (JUICE ONLY)
1 TEASPOON JAMAICA RUM
1 TEASPOON ABRICOTINE
1/2 WINEGLASS SHERRY
1/2 WINEGLASS RYE WHISKEY
1 WHITE OF EGG
USE MIXING GLASS HALF FULL OF ICE, SHAKE THOROUGHLY AND STRAIN INTO PUNCH GLASS. TRIM WITH FRUIT, FILL UP WITH CARBONATED WATER, SPRINKLE WITH NUTMEG.

(Not the one that Bob Fitzsimmons used on Jim Corbett, but it might have done the job as well.)

ASTOR PUNCH

1/2 JIGGER WHITE CREME DE MENTHE POUR OVER A LITTLE SHAVED ICE IN A GOBLET AND ADD 1/2 JIGGER SLOE GIN. DRESS WITH FRUIT AND SERVE.

HAPSBURG PUNCH

1/2 LEMON (JUICE ONLY)
1/3 JIGGER CURACAO
    (OR COINTREAU)
2 OUNCES FINE WHISKEY
STIR IN A HIGHBALL GLASS
FILLED WITH CRUSHED ICE,
DECORATE WITH FRUIT.

(Did this cause the fall of the Hapsburgs?)

AIR MAIL

1 LIME (JUICE ONLY)
1 TEASPOON STRAINED HONEY
1 JIGGER FINE RUM
SHAKE WELL WITH CRACKED ICE
AND STRAIN INTO HIGHBALL GLASS,
FILL WITH CHAMPAGNE.

(It ought to make you fly high.)

FIRST REGIMENT PUNCH

1 PONY IRISH WHISKEY
1 PONY SCOTCH WHISKEY
1 TEASPOON POWDERED SUGAR
3 DASHES LEMON JUICE
2 JIGGERS PIPING HOT WATER

(Ah! For a cold winter night, an open fireplace, and one of these.)

ZOMBIE
—ONE TO A CUSTOMER!

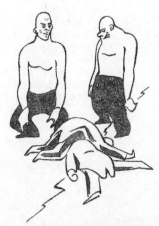

3/4 OUNCE HEAVY-BODIED RUM
    (ABOUT 96 PROOF)
3/4 OUNCE DARK PORTO RICAN RUM
3/4 OUNCE LIGHT PORTO RICAN RUM
3/4 OUNCE RED RUM
1/2 OUNCE APRICOT BRANDY
3/4 OUNCE PINEAPPLE JUICE
1 LARGE LIME (JUICE ONLY)
1 TEASPOON BROWN SUGAR
SHAKE WELL WITH ICE AND POUR
INTO ZOMBIE GLASS WITHOUT
STRAINING. ADD MORE ICE IF
NECESSARY TO FILL GLASS, AND
FLOAT A DASH OF 151 PROOF RUM
ON TOP. GARNISH WITH MINT,
PINEAPPLE AND CHERRIES.

(Perhaps it would be wise to locate the coroner before serving this.)

THE FRENCHMAN LOVES HIS NATIVE WINE;
    THE GERMAN LOVES HIS BEER;
THE ENGLISHMAN LOVES HIS 'ALF AND 'ALF,
    BECAUSE IT BRINGS GOOD CHEER.
THE IRISHMAN LOVES HIS WHISKEY STRAIGHT,
    BECAUSE IT GIVES HIM "DIZZINESS";
THE AMERICAN HAS NO CHOICE AT ALL,
    SO HE DRINKS THE WHOLE D——— BUSINESS.

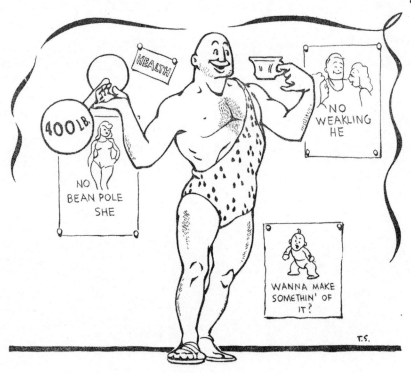

Food For Drink—Not Thought

T HE next family of drinks with which you are likely to have a convivial acquaintance is distinguished by the fact that it offers food values as its principal reason for existence.

It includes the Fizzes, Flips, Eggnogs, Milk Punches, and the like. With just a few exceptions (such as the common Gin Fizz and its sweeter sister, the Sloe Gin Fizz, also the Rum Swizzle, the Lemon Squash, and the Gin Beauty) all in this group boast of containing either eggs or milk—and sometimes both—and for that reason can invariably poll a heavy vote in a popularity contest.

Perhaps a very considerable number of their partisans use their egg and milk content simply as an excuse for getting the hard liquors that go along, but this will always be a moot question. However, many mild drinkers really like the smooth blandness of the egg and milk concoctions, furthermore, the medical fraternity is prone to plug for them as "builder-uppers" in disguise. And so they will always "go over big."

Some of the most famous drinks known to the world of spirits— liquid spirits, of course—come under this heading. First there are the various Eggnogs. Many of these run on the straight whiskey ticket, and others are aligned with the Rum-Brandy Coalition Party, but they are all Eggnogs when it comes to the final analysis. And we find here the Tom and Jerrys—possibly it would be more grammatical to say Toms and Jerrys—and the biggest vote getter of all, if the election could be confined to New Orleans, the justly famous Ramos Gin Fizz. All these and many more you will find on the following pages.

RAMOS FIZZ
or NEW ORLEANS FIZZ

1/2 LEMON (JUICE ONLY)
1/2 TABLESPOON POWDERED SUGAR
1 WHITE OF EGG
1 JIGGER DRY GIN
1 DASH ORANGE JUICE
1 TABLESPOON SWEET CREAM
SHAKE HARD AND LONG WITH CRACKED ICE, STRAIN INTO SMALL HIGHBALL GLASS AND ADD CARBONATED WATER.

(There you have one of the best reasons for New Orleans' fame.)

DERBY FIZZ

1 JIGGER FINE WHISKEY
5 DASHES LEMON JUICE
1 TEASPOON POWDERED SUGAR
1 EGG
3 DASHES CURACAO
SHAKE WELL WITH CRACKED ICE, STRAIN INTO SMALL HIGHBALL GLASS AND FILL WITH CARBONATED WATER.

(A winner at Louisville, where it was first mixed.)

MORNING GLORY FIZZ

1/2 LEMON (JUICE ONLY)
1/2 TABLESPOON POWDERED SUGAR
1 WHITE OF EGG
2 DASHES PERNOD
1 JIGGER FINE WHISKEY
SHAKE WELL WITH CRACKED ICE AND STRAIN INTO SMALL HIGHBALL GLASS. FILL WITH CARBONATED WATER.

(And the morn—in all its glory—may find you still drinking them.)

GIN FIZZ

1/2 LEMON (JUICE ONLY)
1/2 TABLESPOON POWDERED SUGAR
1 JIGGER DRY GIN
ADD CRACKED ICE AND SHAKE THOROUGHLY, STRAIN INTO SMALL HIGHBALL GLASS AND FILL WITH CARBONATED WATER.

ROYAL FIZZ

1/2 LEMON (JUICE ONLY)
1/2 TABLESPOON POWDERED SUGAR
1 JIGGER DRY GIN
1 WHOLE EGG
SHAKE WELL WITH CRACKED ICE, STRAIN INTO SMALL HIGHBALL GLASS, FILL WITH CARBONATED WATER.

Silver Fizz

Made the same as Royal Fizz, using only the white of the one egg.

Golden Fizz

Also the same as Royal Fizz, using only the yolk of the one egg.

Brandy Fizz

1 teaspoon sugar
1/2 lemon (juice only)
1 wineglass Brandy
2 dashes white of egg
Shake well with cracked ice, strain into small highball glass, fill with carbonated water and serve at once.

Sloe Gin Fizz

3 dashes lemon juice
1/2 tablespoon sugar
1 jigger Sloe Gin
Add shaved ice, shake well and strain into small highball glass. Fill with carbonated water and serve while it is effervescing.

Cream Fizz

1 pony lemon juice
1 teaspoon sugar
1 jigger Dry Gin
1/2 jigger fresh cream
Shake well with ice, strain into 8 ounce glass, fill with charged water and serve at once.

Orange Fizz

1 jigger Dry Gin
1/2 orange (juice only)
1/2 teaspoon powdered sugar
Add cracked ice, shake well and strain into small highball glass. Add charged water and serve at once.

Bird of Paradise Fizz

1 jigger Dry Gin
1/2 lemon (juice only)
1 white of egg
3 dashes Grenadine
Shake well with shaved ice, strain into 6 oz. glass and fill with carbonated water.

EGG NOG
Irwin Cobb's

1 WHOLE EGG
1/2 TABLESPOON POWDERED SUGAR
1 JIGGER WHISKEY
1/2 TUMBLER SWEET MILK
SEPERATE YOLK AND BEAT WELL,
STIR IN SUGAR, WHISKEY AND
MILK SEPERATELY. WHIP IN
STIFFLY BEATEN EGG WHITE AND
SERVE WITH NUTMEG ON TOP.

(Mr. Cobb says it will make any man feel like Santa Claus.)

SOUTHERN EGGNOG

1 WHOLE EGG
1 HEAPING TEASPOON SUGAR
1/3 JIGGER JAMAICA RUM
2/3 JIGGER BRANDY
USE LARGE BAR GLASS, ADD FINE
ICE AND FRESH MILK TO FILL,
SHAKE LONG AND WELL. STRAIN
INTO A TALL THIN GLASS AND
SPRINKLE WITH NUTMEG.

BALTIMORE EGGNOG
Note the Madeira.

1 YOLK OF EGG
3/4 TABLESPOON SUGAR
1 PINCH NUTMEG
1 PINCH GROUND CINNAMON
BEAT THE ABOVE INTO A
CREAM AND THEN ADD:
1/2 PONY JAMAICA RUM
3/4 JIGGER MADEIRA WINE
1/4 JIGGER BRANDY
3 CUBES ICE
SHAKE THESE WELL AND POUR
INTO A LARGE BAR GLASS. FILL
WITH MILK AND TOP WITH NUTMEG.

SHERRY EGGNOG

1 WHOLE EGG
1 TABLESPOON SUGAR
1 PONY BRANDY
1 WINEGLASS SHERRY
SHAKE WELL WITH FINE ICE,
STRAIN INTO FANCY BAR GLASS
AND SERVE WITH NUTMEG ON
TOP.

CIDER EGGNOG

1 WHOLE EGG
1 TABLESPOON POWDERED SUGAR
1/2 PINT MILK
SHAKE WELL WITH CRACKED ICE,
STRAIN INTO A TOM COLLINS
GLASS AND ADD 1 JIGGER SWEET
CIDER. STIR WELL AND TOP WITH
NUTMEG.

RUM SWIZZLE

1/4 LIME (JUICE ONLY)
1/2 LEMON (JUICE ONLY)
1 LARGE DASH ANGOSTURA BITTERS
1 BARSPOON POWDERED SUGAR
1 JIGGER FINE RUM
PLACE ALL THESE IN 10 OZ. THIN
GLASS ALREADY FULL OF SHAVED
ICE, STIR WELL AND FILL WITH
CARBONATED WATER.

MOJITO

1 TEASPOON POWDERED SUGAR
1/2 LIME (JUICE ONLY)
1 JIGGER FINE RUM
PLACE THESE IN TALL HIGHBALL
GLASS ALONG WITH QUANTITY OF
SHAVED ICE. FILL WITH SELTZER
WATER, STIR WELL, ADD SOME
MINT LEAVES AND A TWIST OF
LEMON PEEL JUST BEFORE SERVING.

BRANDY FLIP

1 FRESH EGG
1 DESSERT SPOON POWDERED SUGAR
1 JIGGER BRANDY
USE MEDIUM MIXING GLASS AND
SHAKE WELL WITH CRACKED ICE.
STRAIN INTO FANCY GLASS AND
GRATE A LITTLE NUTMEG ON TOP.

(You'll flip, too, if you go too far with this.)

GIN FLIP

MADE THE SAME AS BRANDY FLIP,
USING HOLLAND GIN INSTEAD OF
BRANDY.

WHISKEY FLIP

MADE THE SAME AS BRANDY FLIP,
EXCEPT THAT WHISKEY IS USED
INSTEAD OF BRANDY.

PORT WINE FLIP

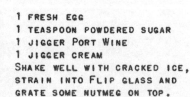

1 FRESH EGG
1 TEASPOON POWDERED SUGAR
1 JIGGER PORT WINE
1 JIGGER CREAM
SHAKE WELL WITH CRACKED ICE,
STRAIN INTO FLIP GLASS AND
GRATE SOME NUTMEG ON TOP.

HERE'S TO YOU, AS GOOD AS YOU ARE,
  AND TO ME, AS BAD AS I AM;
AS GOOD AS YOU ARE, AND AS BAD AS I AM;
  I'M AS GOOD AS YOU ARE, AS BAD AS I AM.

CLARET FLIP

1 FRESH EGG
1 TABLESPOON POWDERED SUGAR
3 OUNCES CLARET
SHAKE HARD IN MIXING GLASS WITH
CRACKED ICE, STRAIN INTO PUNCH
GLASS AND TOP WITH GRATED NUTMEG.

SHERRY FLIP

1 FRESH EGG
1 DESSERT SPOON POWDERED SUGAR
1 WINEGLASS SHERRY
SHAKE WELL WITH CRACKED ICE IN
SMALL MIXING GLASS, STRAIN INTO
FLIP GLASS, GRATE NUTMEG ON TOP
AND SERVE.

ALE FLIP
It's English, you know.

POUR ALE INTO REGULAR ALE GLASS
TO NEAR THE TOP, ADD 1 TEASPOON
SUGAR AND BREAK IN 1 EGG. STIR
WELL AND SPRINKLE WITH NUTMEG.

BRACE UP

1 TABLESPOON POWDERED SUGAR
3 DASHES ANGOSTURA BITTERS
3 DASHES LEMON JUICE
1 DASH LIME JUICE
2 DASHES ANISETTE
1 WHOLE EGG
3/4 WINEGLASS BRANDY
SHAKE WELL WITH SHAVED ICE,
STRAIN INTO LARGE GLASS AND
FILL WITH CARBONATED WATER.

DREAM

1 TEASPOON SUGAR
4 DASHES LEMON JUICE
1 WHITE OF EGG
1 JIGGER TOM GIN
1 WINEGLASS MILK OR CREAM
SHAKE WELL WITH CRACKED ICE,
STRAIN INTO THIN LEMONADE
GLASS, FLOAT CREME DE MENTHE
ON TOP.

(And why shouldn't you dream?)

KHEDIVE

1 PONY SLOE GIN
1 PONY RYE
1/2 LEMON (JUICE AND RIND)
1 DASH RASPBERRY SYRUP
1 TABLESPOON SUGAR
1 DASH FRESH CREAM
1 WHOLE EGG
SHAKE WELL, STRAIN INTO A
FIZZ GLASS AND FILL WITH
SELTZER.

GIN BEAUTY
All its name implies.

1 JIGGER DRY GIN
1/2 LEMON (JUICE ONLY)
1/2 TEASPOON GRENADINE
1/2 TABLESPOON POWDERED SUGAR
SHAKE WELL WITH CRACKED ICE,
STRAIN INTO TOM COLLINS GLASS,
FILL WITH SODA AND TOP WITH
A SPRIG OF FRESH MINT.

PEACH BLOW FIZZ
Sounds good!

1 JIGGER DRY GIN
1/2 LEMON (JUICE ONLY)
1 TABLESPOON SUGAR
1 TABLESPOON GRENADINE
1 TEASPOON FRESH CREAM
SHAKE WELL WITH CRACKED ICE,
STRAIN INTO BAR GLASS AND
FILL WITH SODA.

RUBY FIZZ

1 TEASPOON SUGAR
1/2 LEMON (JUICE ONLY)
1 JIGGER SLOE GIN
1 WHOLE EGG
SHAKE WELL WITH CRACKED ICE,
THEN POUR ICE AND ALL INTO
TALL GLASS AND FILL WITH
GINGER ALE.

(This one has possibilities, what say you?)

IMPERIAL

1 PONY FINE WHISKEY
1/2 PONY RUM
1/2 TABLESPOON SUGAR
1/2 LEMON (JUICE ONLY)
SHAKE WELL WITH CRACKED ICE,
STRAIN INTO MEDIUM SIZE GLASS
AND FILL WITH CARBONATED WATER.

LEMON SQUASH

SQUEEZE 1/2 LEMON AND 1/2 LIME
AND PUT BOTH RINDS AND JUICE
INTO A GLASS BEER STEIN. ADD
2 OUNCES FINE WHISKEY, 1 TEA-
SPOON POWDERED SUGAR AND SOME
SHAVED ICE. FILL WITH SELTZER
AND SUBMERGE TWO SPRIGS OF
FRESH MINT. (DO NOT CRUSH.)

*(They say it's wonderful after a hard game of tennis.
Always did say that game had its points.)*

'TIS PITY WINE SHOULD BE SO DELETERIOUS,
    FOR TEA AND COFFEE LEAVE US MUCH MORE SERIOUS.
           — BYRON'S "DON JUAN"

HOT EGGNOG

1 WHOLE EGG
1 TABLESPOON SUGAR
1 WINEGLASS BRANDY
1/2 WINEGLASS JAMAICA RUM
WHIP THE ABOVE TOGETHER IN
HEAVY GLASS, STIR HOT MILK
INTO SAME AND DO IT THOROUGHLY.
TOP WITH NUTMEG.

GENERAL HARRISON EGGNOG

1 FRESH EGG
1 TEASPOON SUGAR
3 CUBES ICE
FILL GLASS WITH SWEET CIDER,
SHAKE WELL, AND SERVE AT ONCE.

(Maybe they should have nicknamed him "Old Tipsycanoe.")

SOLO EGGNOG

BREAK 1 FRESH EGG INTO A
LARGE GLASS, ADD 2 TEASPOONS
POWDERED SUGAR, 1 WINEGLASS
MILK, AND FILL GLASS WITH
HOT RUM. MIX WELL AND TOP
WITH A DASH OF ANGOSTURA
BITTERS.

(They call it Solo because it makes you feel so high.)

TOM & JERRY

1 WHOLE EGG
1/2 JIGGER JAMAICA RUM
1 TEASPOON POWDERED SUGAR
1/4 TEASPOON POWDERED ALLSPICE
1/4 OUNCE BRANDY
MIX TOGETHER YOLK OF EGG, RUM,
SUGAR AND ALLSPICE, THEN ADD
WHITE OF EGG (BEATEN TO A STIFF
FROTH) AND BRANDY. DIVIDE THIS
EQUALLY IN TWO TOM & JERRY MUGS,
ADD 1/2 JIGGER BRANDY TO EACH,
STIR PIPING HOT WATER OR MILK
INTO SAME AND TOP WITH NUTMEG.

RUM MILK PUNCH

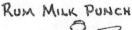

1 YOLK OF EGG
1 TABLESPOON SUGAR
BEAT THESE TOGETHER THOROUGHLY
AND THEN STIR INTO A GLASS OF
HOT MILK. ADD 1 JIGGER OF
CHOICE RUM AND SPRINKLE NUTMEG
ON TOP.

(Be sure that it is hot, and you won't need to worry about the punch—you'll get it straight from the shoulder!)

HOT LOCOMOTIVE
It goes places—and how!

1 WHOLE EGG
1/2 TABLESPOON SUGAR
1 PONY STRAINED HONEY
STIR THESE AND ADD:
1/2 PONY CURACAO
1½ WINEGLASS BURGUNDY
   (OR CLARET)
PLACE ALL IN COOKING DISH
AND BRING TO BOIL. POUR INTO
MUG, ADD SLICE OF LEMON AND
A LITTLE CINNAMON.

HUMPTY DUMPTY

1/2 TABLESPOON SUGAR
1 WHOLE EGG
3/4 WINEGLASS BRANDY
1/4 WINEGLASS JAMAICA RUM
ADD ICE AND MILK TO FILL
MIXING GLASS, SHAKE WELL,
STRAIN INTO LARGE PUNCH GLASS
AND SPRINKLE WITH NUTMEG.

(You've heard about Humpty Dumpty's fall, so be careful.)

MILK PUNCH

1 TUMBLER SWEET MILK
1 TABLESPOON POWDERED SUGAR
1 JIGGER WHISKEY
SHAKE WELL WITH CRACKED ICE,
STRAIN INTO HIGHBALL GLASS AND
SPRINKLE NUTMEG ON TOP.

KAFFIR'S DREAM
From Africa, this one.

1 PONY SLOE GIN
1 PONY RYE
1 DASH RASPBERRY SYRUP
1/2 TABLESPOON SUGAR
1 WHOLE EGG
1 DASH FRESH CREAM
SHAKE WELL AND STRAIN INTO
LARGE WINEGLASS.

WHITE PLUSH

2/3 JIGGER RYE
1/3 JIGGER MARASCHINO
1 WHOLE EGG
1/2 PINT FRESH CREAM
SHAKE WELL WITH ICE, STRAIN
INTO A THIN GLASS.

("Plush" sounds soft—for HARD *liqour.)*

" COME, SEND ROUND THE WINE, AND LEAVE POINTS
OF BELIEF TO SIMPLETON SAGES AND REASONING
FOOLS."
        – THOMAS MOORE

Mixed Drinks—But Not Mixed

WE come now to the smallest and most exclusive little group in all the mixed drink family. Its members are strictly limited to the Pousse Cafes, so it is what might be called a very close corporation. There are no others like them, so they get ranking as a class all by themselves.

Their name is derived from two French words. The first is *pousser*, meaning to push, and the second is *cafe,* meaning coffee, so a literal translation is "to push coffee." They are usually served right after coffee, so the reason for the name is obvious.

Strictly speaking, Pousse Cafes are not really mixed drinks at all. At least they are not mixed when served, though it is quite probable they will be mixed on introduction to the inner man. But when being prepared "to set before the king" it is of prime importance that the ingredients shall not be mixed.

They usually consist of several cordials or liqueurs of different specific gravities (sometimes an entirely foreign constituent like cream or an egg is introduced, but not often). The various cordials are added so carefully to the Pousse Cafe glass that each floats on top of the one just before it. In other words:

"When is a mixed drink not a mixed drink?" When it is a Pousse Cafe.

Some of the most popular of these un-mixed drinks are given here.

POUSSE CAFE

1/6 MARASCHINO
1/6 RASPBERRY SYRUP
1/6 CREME DE CACAO
1/6 CURACAO
1/6 BRANDY
USE A LIQUEUR GLASS FOR THIS.
THE TRICK IS TO POUR THESE SO
CAREFULLY THAT THE LIQUEURS
DO NOT MIX.

AMERICAN POUSSE CAFE

1/5 MARASCHINO
1/5 CURACAO
1/5 GREEN CHARTREUSE
1/5 ANISETTE
1/5 BRANDY
KEEP THE COLORS SEPERATE. SET
FIRE TO THE BRANDY, ALLOW TO
BLAZE A MOMENT, EXTINGUISH WITH
BOTTOM OF ANOTHER GLASS.

SANTINA'S POUSSE CAFE

USE SHERRY GLASS.
1/2 PONY BRANDY
1/2 PONY MARASCHINO
1/2 PONY CURACAO
1/2 PONY JAMAICA RUM

(This is another famous drink that was born at Santina's in New Oreleans, before the Civil War.)

KNICKERBEIN OR BISMARCK

USE BELL SHERRY GLASS AND POUR
INGREDIENTS CAREFULLY.
1/2 GLASS MARASCHINO
1 YOLK OF EGG
ENOUGH BENEDICTINE TO SURROUND
EGG, ALMOST FILL GLASS WITH
KUMMEL, ADD 3 DROPS ANGOSTURA
BITTERS AND SERVE.

(Let them guess how to drink this one—we can't tell you.)

BRANDY CHAMPARELLE

USE SMALL WINEGLASS.
1/3 RED CURACAO
1/3 ANISETTE, MARASCHINO OR
        YELLOW CHARTREUSE
1/3 BRANDY
1 DASH ANGOSTURA BITTERS

GOLDEN SLIPPER

1 JIGGER YELLOW CHARTREUSE
1 YOLK OF EGG
1 JIGGER DANZIGER GOLDWASSER
USE LARGE WINEGLASS. DO NOT
BREAK THE YOLK OF EGG.

(Famous in the Gay Nineties as a ladies' drink.)

CAPE COD RAINBOW

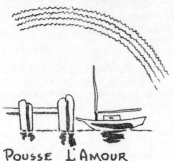

USE LARGE GLASS, FILLED WITH
CRACKED ICE.
2 OUNCES GIN
1 PONY ORANGE JUICE
1 DASH GRENADINE (ALLOW THIS
    TO SETTLE AT THE BOTTOM)
1 TABLESPOON GREEN CREME DE MENTHE
    (LAID CAREFULLY ON TOP)
1 TWIST LEMON PEEL.

*(Now we know why some people are "forever
chasing rainbows.")*

POUSSE L'AMOUR

USE SHERRY GLASS.
1/5 CREME DE VANILLE
1 YOLK OF EGG
POUR IN ENOUGH MARASCHINO TO
COVER THE YOLK, FILL GLASS
WITH COGNAC.

(Something like a kiss in the dark.)

STARS & STRIPES

1/3 GRENADINE
1/3 WHITE CREME DE MENTHE
1/3 CREME DE VIOLETTE

(You don't wave this—you drink it.)

ANGEL'S KISS

1/4 CREME DE CACAO
1/4 PRINELLE
1/4 CREME DE VIOLETTE
1/4 SWEET CREAM

BRANDY SCAFFA

1/3 MARASCHINO
1/3 GREEN CHARTREUSE
1/3 BRANDY
POUR THESE CAREFULLY INTO A
SMALL WINEGLASS, DO NOT STIR.

BACHELOR'S DREAM

1/2 PONY CURACAO
1/2 PONY MARASCHINO
1/2 PONY CREME DE VIOLETTE
1/2 PONY RICH CREAM
POUR THESE IN SLOWLY, SO THEY
WILL NOT MIX.

(Can't see why it should be reserved for single men.)

ECLIPSE

1/2 LEMON (JUICE ONLY)
1/2 PONY DRY GIN
1 PONY SLOE GIN
SHAKE THESE WELL WITH SHAVED
ICE. PUT AN OLIVE IN A LARGE
COCKTAIL GLASS AND POUR IN
ENOUGH GRENADINE TO COVER.
INTO THIS STRAIN CONTENTS OF
YOUR SHAKER, POURING SLOWLY
SO AS NOT TO MIX WITH THE
GRENADINE.

Repeating Some Cocktails

NO treatise on the subject of mixed drinks could possibly go
before the public without a section devoted to that most popular class of all, the Cocktail, but we have previously devoted a
whole book to this rich subject (see "Just Cocktails," published
in October, 1939). In this book we covered the whole field of
this most American of all drinks thoroughly and completely. (Over
350 were listed.)

Yet, we feel that this more general work should not overlook the
Cocktail entirely. That being the case, it was considered best from
all angles that a small, carefully selected group of the more widely
known and more commonly served of "Just Cocktails" be given
again, thus covering all the everyday needs of the amateur "mixologist."

So the thirty-odd that would probably poll the heaviest votes are
herein reprinted from "Just Cocktails."

DAIQUIRI

JUICE OF 1 LIME
1 TEASPOON POWDERED SUGAR
1 JIGGER JAMAICA RUM

OLD FASHIONED

1 JIGGER BOURBON
2 DASHES ANGOSTURA BITTERS
1/2 LUMP SUGAR
2 TEASPOONS WATER
STIR WELL, ADD CUBE OF ICE
AND PIECES OF LEMON AND ORANGE.

MANHATTAN
No. 1 in hit parade.

1/2 RYE WHISKEY
1/2 ITALIAN VERMOUTH
1 DASH ORANGE BITTERS
SERVE WITH A MARASCHINO CHERRY.

GIN

1 JIGGER DRY GIN
3 DASHES BITTERS
1 TWIST LEMON PEEL

MARTINI

1/2 TOM GIN
1/2 ITALIAN VERMOUTH
1 DASH ORANGE BITTERS
SERVE WITH A GREEN OLIVE.

DRY MARTINI

2/3 DRY GIN
1/3 FRENCH VERMOUTH
1 DASH BITTERS
TWIST OF LEMON PEEL ON
TOP. SERVE WITH GREEN OLIVE.

PRESIDENT'S,
CUBAN

1 PONY RUM
1 PONY CURACAO
1 PONY FRENCH VERMOUTH
2 DASHES GRENADINE
SERVE WITH A CHERRY AND
ORANGE PEEL.

ALEXANDER

1 PONY DRY GIN
1 PONY CREME DE CACAO
1 PONY FRESH CREAM

MILLIONAIRE

1/3 JAMAICA RUM
1/3 APRICOT BRANDY
1/3 SLOE GIN
1 LIME (JUICE ONLY)
1 DASH GRENADINE

BRANDY

1 JIGGER BEST BRANDY
2 DASHES BITTERS
1 DASH ITALIAN VERMOUTH
1 TWIST LEMON PEEL

DUBONNET

1/2 DUBONNET
1/2 DRY GIN

COGNAC

1/3 COGNAC
1/3 COINTREAU
1/3 LEMON JUICE

CHAMPAGNE
A star in the movies.

1/3 GLASS CRACKED ICE
1 LUMP SUGAR
2 DASHES ANGOSTURA BITTERS
1 SLICE ORANGE
PUT ALL THESE IN 5 OUNCE
CHAMPAGNE GOBLET, FILL WITH
CHAMPAGNE. STIR GENTLY.

WHISKEY

1 JIGGER WHISKEY
4 DASHES SYRUP
1 DASH BITTERS

SLOE GIN

2/3 SLOE GIN
1/3 PLYMOUTH GIN
1 DASH ORANGE BITTERS

BRONX
Not the cheer.

1 JIGGER DRY GIN
1/2 JIGGER FRENCH VERMOUTH
1/2 JIGGER ITALIAN VERMOUTH
ADD JUICE OF 1/4 ORANGE AND
SHAKE WELL. SERVE WITH SLICE
OF ORANGE.

VERMOUTH

1 JIGGER FRENCH VERMOUTH
1 DASH ABSINTHE
1 DASH MARASCHINO
2 DASHES BITTERS
SERVE WITH A CHERRY.

BACARDI

1 JIGGER BACARDI RUM
1/2 LIME (JUICE ONLY)
2 DASHES GRENADINE

ABSINTHE

1 PONY ABSINTHE
1 PONY WATER
2 DASHES BITTERS
3 DASHES BENEDICTINE

ORANGE BLOSSOM
Pretty good!

1/3 TOM GIN
1/3 ITALIAN VERMOUTH
1/3 ORANGE JUICE

JACK ROSE

2/3 APPLEJACK
1/3 GRENADINE
1 LIME (JUICE ONLY)

CLOVER CLUB

1 JIGGER GIN
3 DASHES RASPBERRY SYRUP
1 WHITE OF EGG
1/2 TEASPOON SUGAR
1/2 LEMON (JUICE ONLY)
SHAKE WELL WITH ICE.

COFFEE

2/3 PORT WINE
1/3 BRANDY
1 YOLK OF EGG
1 TEASPOON SUGAR

PINK LADY
Lots of style.

1/3 GIN
1/3 LIME JUICE
1/3 APPLEJACK
2 DASHES GRENADINE

STINGER

1/2 WHITE CREME DE MENTHE
1/2 BRANDY

SIDE CAR

2/3 BRANDY
1/3 COINTREAU
1 DASH LIME JUICE

SAZERAC
Pride of New Orleans.

1 JIGGER BOURBON
  (OR SCOTCH)
1 DASH ABSINTHE (PERNOD)
1 DASH ITALIAN VERMOUTH
ADD A FEW DASHES OF
PEYCHAND BITTERS.

WARD EIGHT

1/2 BOURBON WHISKEY
1/4 LEMON JUICE
1/4 ORANGE JUICE
1 DASH GRENADINE

LONE TREE

1/2 TOM GIN
1/4 ITALIAN VERMOUTH
1/4 FRENCH VERMOUTH

RUM MANHATTAN

1 JIGGER RUM
1/2 JIGGER ITALIAN VERMOUTH
1 DASH BITTERS

COME FILL A FRESH BUMPER,
FOR WHY SHOULD WE GO,
WHILE THE NECTAR STILL REDDENS
OUR CUPS AS THEY FLOW.
POUR OUT THE RICH JUICES;
STILL BRIGHT WITH THE SUN;
'TILL O'ER THE BRIMMED CRYSTAL
THE RUBIES SHALL RUN.
          — OLIVER WENDELL HOLMES

Ending With "Party Mixes"

ALL the creations of the drink mixer's skill placed before you up to now have been for solo portions, one joy producer for one man. But there are many occasions when a liquid structure that will withstand the attacks of ten or a dozen or even fifty of your thirst maddened friends must be prepared.

The celebration of Christmas or the Year's birthday, the return of the Prodigal Son, or the departure of the Nuptialed Daughter, the arrival of twins to increase your liabilities, or the addition of an unexpected inheritance to your assets; any of these possibilities and scores of others call for you to know something about a "Party Mix," a bunch of libations all stirred up in one.

And so it is quite probable that the collection of mixed drinks with which we now round off this modest work may be consulted more often than any of those that have gone before. The general term of "Party Mixes" should do very well to designate this group. It includes many tempting mixtures that have furnished the finishing touches to even historic events, also simpler but just as satisfying bowls of elixir that can warm the cockles of our hearts on every day occasions.

Here again we will meet such friends of other pages as the Eggnog, the Tom and Jerry, and the Champagne Punch, but this time the proportions are to satisfy the first, second, and third person, plural. Among these you will find some hoary ancients like the Huckle-My-Butt and the Rumfustian of Old England, and rubbing elbows with these you will see that triumph of our own ante-bellum days, the Bellevue Eggnog. And for the very modern drinker there are the Honolulu Surprise and that liquid K. O., the Zombie. These are "hot off the griddle."

Browse among these generously planned liquid masterpieces—you will find them more interesting and far more tempting than the solo variety. Here's happy days!

CHRISTMAS EGGNOG
For 10 guests.

BEAT THE WHITES OF 6 EGGS UNTIL STIFF AND ADD 1 LEVEL CUP OF POWDERED SUGAR. WHIP THE YOLKS TO A FROTH AND STIR THEM SLOWLY INTO THE WHITES. POUR IN 1/4 CUP JAMAICA RUM AND 1 PINT FINE WHISKEY, FOLLOWED BY 1 PINT MILK AND 1 PINT RICH CREAM, STIRRING GENTLY ALL THE WHILE. POUR INTO CUPS AND SPRINKLE WITH NUTMEG.

(After two or three drinks of this, you will vote for Christmas to come every week.)

BELLEVUE EGGNOG
Serves 12 generously.

BEAT THE YOLKS OF 12 FRESH EGGS AND 12 TABLESPOONS OF GRANULATED SUGAR TOGETHER, ADDING THE LATTER IN SMALL QUANTITIES. WHEN SMOOTH POUR IN A GENEROUS PINT OF EXTRA FINE COGNAC (THIS MUST BE GOOD IF YOU WANT YOUR DRINK TO EARN ITS DUE PRAISE). ADD THE COGNAC SLOWLY AND STIR ALL THE TIME, THEN POUR IN A SCANT HALF PINT OF HEAVY-BODIED RUM, STILL SLOWLY AND STILL STIRRING. ADD A PINT OF RICH MILK AND A HALF PINT OF HEAVY CREAM IN SAME MANNER. NOW BEAT THE EGG WHITES UNTIL VERY STIFF AND WHIP INTO THE ABOVE MIXTURE, TOGETHER WITH A GRATED NUTMEG. CHILL THOROUGHLY BY SETTING THE BOWL IN SNOWBANK, OR A MODERN REFRIGERATOR WILL DO.

(The gods of Olympus would have had no use for nectar if they had tasted this first.)

TOM AND JERRY
For a round dozen.

SEPERATE 12 FRESH EGGS, BEAT YOLKS UNTIL SMOOTH, ADDING 3 TABLESPOONS OF POWDERED SUGAR AND TWO SCANT TEASPOONS OF GRATED NUTMEG. NOW ADD 6 JIGGERS JAMAICA RUM, BEAT WHITES UNTIL STIFF AND WHIP INTO THE MIXTURE, AND ADD 3 JIGGERS BRANDY. DIVIDE THIS INTO 12 MUGS AND FILL THEM WITH BOILING HOT WATER OR HOT MILK.

(A grand drink for a cold day—no wonder so many people like winter.)

BRANDY PUNCH
Plenty for twenty.

3 QUARTS BRANDY
1/2 PINT JAMAICA RUM
1 GALLON WATER
6 LEMONS (JUICE ONLY)
1 GILL CURACAO
MIX THE LIQUORS AND POUR INTO
PUNCH BOWL CONTAINING LARGE
PIECE OF ICE. ADD LEMON JUICE,
WATER AND ENOUGH SUGAR TO
SWEETEN. NEXT PUT IN 3 ORANGES,
SLICED, A DICED PINEAPPLE AND
1/2 PINT RASPBERRIES. LET STAND
UNTIL THOROUGHLY CHILLED.

(It's a drink you can remember—if you CAN *remember.)*

CHAMPAGNE PUNCH
As served in Rheins, France.

1/4 POUND POWDERED SUGAR
1 GLASS BRANDY
1 QUART CURACAO
1 GLASS MARASCHINO
1 QUART MINERAL WATER
2 QUARTS CHAMPAGNE
MIX THESE IN A PUNCH BOWL
THAT IS SET IN A BANK OF
ICE. DECORATE WITH FRESH
FRUITS, AND ADD A SPIRAL
OF CUCUMBER RIND FOR A
DISTINCTIVE AND UNIQUE FLAVOR.

DIAMOND COCKTAILS
For a quartette.

1 LIME (JUICE ONLY)
1 LEMON (JUICE ONLY)
1 ORANGE (JUICE ONLY)
4 TABLESPOONS RASPBERRY SYRUP
1 WINEGLASS GIN
STIR AND DIVIDE INTO FOUR TALL
GLASSES FILLED WITH CRACKED ICE.
FILL TO TOP WITH CHAMPAGNE.

FISH CLUB PUNCH
*Popular in the
Gay Nineties.*

1/3 PINT LEMON JUICE
3/4 POUND SUGAR
    (DISSOLVED IN WATER)
1/2 PINT COGNAC
1/4 PINT PEACH BRANDY
1/4 PINT JAMAICA RUM
2½ PINTS COLD WATER
MIX WELL IN A PUNCH BOWL,
SURROUNDED WITH CRACKED ICE.

ONE SIP OF THIS
WILL BATHE THE DROOPING SPIRITS IN DELIGHT
BEYOND THE BLISS OF DREAMS.
— MILTON'S "COMUS"

NEGUS
Named after an admiral.

POUR A PINT OF PORT WINE IN A
BOWL AND ADD TEN LUMPS OF SUGAR
THAT HAVE BEEN RUBBED ON A
LEMON RIND AND THE JUICE OF ONE
WHOLE LEMON. NOW COMES A PINCH
OF GRATED NUTMEG AND A QUART
OF BOILING WATER. STIR AND
SERVE HOT.

APPLEJACK PUNCH
For a small crowd.

1 PINT APPLEJACK
2 LEMONS (JUICE ONLY)
10 LUMPS SUGAR
1 GLASS BRANDY
STIR AND SERVE, ADDING
BOILING WATER IF YOU WANT
IT HOT.

GROG
This smacks of the sea.

1 QUART RUM
1 QUART HOT WATER
1 CUP SUGAR
1 SLICED LEMON
    (IF AVAILABLE AND DESIRED)

HUCKLE-MY-BUTT
An old-timer in England.

1 QUART BEER
1/2 PINT BRANDY
2 WHOLE EGGS (BEATEN)
SUGAR TO TASTE, PINCHES OF
CINNAMON, CLOVES AND NUTMEG.
STIR THOROUGHLY.

LAMB'S WOOL
Just for harvest holidays.

PUT 6 BAKED APPLES IN A LARGE
DISH AND BREAK APPLES SO THE
PULP IS EXPOSED. POUR OVER THESE
1 QUART OF HOT ALE AND SUGAR TO
TASTE. ADD NUTMEG AND GINGER
IN SMALL QUANTITIES.

WASSAIL BOWL
It dates back to Ivanhoe.

PUT 1 POUND OF SUGAR IN A BOWL,
ADD 3 QUARTS OF WARM BEER AND
4 GLASSES OF SHERRY. ADD SOME
GINGER AND NUTMEG AND FLOAT A
SLICE OF LEMON ON TOP.

RUMFUSTIAN
*The end of the hunts-
man's day.*

BEAT THE YOLKS OF 12 EGGS WELL
AND PUT THEM INTO A QUART OF
STRONG BEER. ADD 1 PINT GIN.
NOW POUR 1 QUART SHERRY INTO
A SAUCEPAN, ADD A STICK OF
CINNAMON, A GRATED NUTMEG,
A DOZEN LUMPS OF SUGAR AND
THE RIND OF A LEMON. BRING
THIS TO A BOIL, AND POUR THE
TWO MIXTURES TOGETHER. STIR
AND SERVE HOT.

WHITE TIGER'S MILK
An old English favorite

1 WINEGLASS APPLEJACK
1 WINEGLASS PEACH BRANDY
1/2 TEASPOON AROMATIC TINCTURE
1 WHITE OF EGG (BEATEN STIFF)
1 QUART OF FRESH MILK
POUR ALL THE LIQUORS INTO THE
MILK, FOLD IN THE EGGS SWEETEN
TO TASTE AND SERVE COLD WITH
NUTMEG ON TOP.

(We never heard of a white tiger, but maybe the chap who first drank this saw one— along with some pink elephants.

CORN POPPER HIGHBALL
For party of 10.

1 PINT FINE WHISKEY
1/2 PINT FRESH CREAM
2 WHITES OF EGGS
1 TABLESPOON GRENADINE
STIR THESE TOGETHER BRISKLY.
USE SMALL HIGHBALL GLASSES AND
HALF FILL THEM WITH THIS MIXTURE.
ADD 1 CUBE OF ICE AND FILL WITH
SELTZER.

(Something ought to pop.)

RHEIMS PUNCH
For party of 12.

1/2 CUP POWDERED SUGAR
3 ORANGES (SLICED AND HALVED)
5 LEMONS (JUICE ONLY)
6 SLICES PINEAPPLE, DICED
12 MARASCHINO CHERRIES
PUT ALL THESE INTO A PUNCH
BOWL AND ADD 3 QUARTS OF
CHILLED CHAMPAGNE. ADD
1 QUART OF ORANGE SHERBET,
TO KEEP THE PUNCH COOL

OLD WALDORF PUNCH
It may be old, but the taste is new.

PUT ICE IN A PUNCH BOWL AND ADD:
1 SMALL GLASS BRANDY
1 LIQUEUR GLASS MARASCHINO
1 BARSPOON POWDERED SUGAR
1 QUART CHAMPAGNE
1 PINT CARBONATED WATER
USE PLENTY OF FRUIT IN SEASON
AND MIX WELL.

FRIEND OF MY SOUL, THIS GOBLET SIP -
'TWILL CHASE AWAY THE PENSIVE TEAR;
'TIS NOT AS SWEET AS WOMAN'S LIP,
BUT, OH! 'TIS MORE SINCERE.

CHAMPAGNE BOWLER
Note accent on American products.

1/2 PINT STRAWBERRIES
2 TABLESPOONS POWDERED SUGAR
CRUSH THE BERRIES IN THE SUGAR
AND POUR OVER THEM 2 OUNCES
COGNAC AND 8 OUNCES DOMESTIC
WHITE WINE. LET THIS STAND FOR
ABOUT TWO HOURS. PUT A LARGE
PIECE OF ICE INTO A GOOD SIZE
BOWL AND POUR IN THE STRAWBERRIES.
ADD TWO BOTTLES DOMESTIC WHITE
WINE AND TWO BOTTLES DOMESTIC
CHAMPAGNE. (OTHER FRESH FRUIT IN
SEASON MAY BE USED IN PLACE OF
STRAWBERRIES.)

GLOW WINE
Very cotinental, indeed!

2 BOTTLES RED WINE
1/2 POUND SUGAR
6 CLOVES
1/2 LEMON PEEL
PUT THESE INTO A SAUCE PAN AND
BRING TO BOILING POINT. SERVE
WITH SLICE OF ORANGE.

ARCHBISHOP PUNCH
This reads like the Dark Ages.

STICK CLOVES INTO A GOOD SIZED
ORANGE, AND ROAST IN OVEN UNTIL
SKIN IS BROWN. THEN QUARTER AND
SEED IT, PUT IT IN A SAUCEPAN
AND COVER WITH A BOTTLE OF CLARET.
ADD SUGAR AND LET IT SIMMER OVER
FIRE UNTIL HOT. SERVE IN MUGS,
A QUARTER ORANGE TO EACH MUG,
FILLING IT WITH THE MULLED WINE.

SUN VALLEY
The name stamps it as new.

HEAT A QUART OF RICH CREAM
ALMOST TO THE BOILING POINT, ADD
2 TABLESPOONS POWDERED SUGAR.
BEAT THE YOLKS OF 4 EGGS IN A
LITTLE MILK AND ADD TO THE CREAM.
THEN POUR IN LARGE GLASS JAMAICA
RUM, STIR THOROUGHLY AND SERVE IN
CUPS.

OLD BERLIN CASTLE PUNCH
From the Rhine district.

DISSOLVE TWO POUNDS OF SUGAR IN
A QUART OF WATER. PLACE IN GRANITE
SAUCEPAN AND BRING TO A BOIL, THEN
REDUCE THE HEAT AND ADD 2 BOTTLES
RHINE WINE, KEEPING BELOW BOILING
POINT. SOAK A LUMP OF SUGAR IN
BRANDY AND IGNITE IT, HOLDING IT
IN A SPOON OVER THE PAN. THEN
SLOWLY POUR A PINT OF GOOD RUM
OVER THE BURNING SUGAR AND INTO
THE PAN. SERVE PIPING HOT.

HOT WINE PUNCH

A Parisian welcome to guests.

TO ONE HALF PINT BOILING WATER,
ADD THE FOLLOWING INGREDIENTS:
3 TABLESPOONS SUGAR
6 CLOVES
3 PIECES STICK CINNAMON
1 RIND OF LEMON
WHILE THIS MIXTURE IS BOILING
POUR IN 1 QUART GOOD CLARET OR
BURGUNDY, AND SERVE HOT.

SCOTCH PUNCH

A Highland favorite after the hunt. ....

INTO A STONE JUG (ONE THAT CAN
BE SEALED) POUR 2 QUARTS SCOTCH
WHISKEY AND 1 QUART BEST BRANDY.
BREW A CUP OF GREEN TEA, MEDIUM
STRENGTH, POUR INTO JAR, THEN ADD
6 LEMON RINDS
1 TEASPOON CLOVES
1 TABLESPOON ALLSPICE
30 LUMPS SUGAR
SEAL THE JUG AND ALLOW TO STAND
AT LEAST SIX WEEKS IN A COOL
PLACE. SERVE EITHER HOT OR COLD.

BOMBAY PUNCH

Described as a royal concotion.

1 QUART COGNAC
1 QUART SHERRY
1/4 PINT MARASCHINO
1/4 PINT ORANGE CURACAO
2 QUARTS CARBONATED WATER
4 QUARTS CHAMPAGNE
HAVE PUNCH BOWL SET IN BANK OF
ICE, NONE INSIDE, THEN DECORATE
WITH FRUITS.

SAUTERNES PUNCH

Guaranteed to lower the thermometer.

1 QUART SAUTERNES
1 PINT MINERAL WATER
2 OUNCES COGNAC
1 OUNCE ORANGE CURACAO
1 OUNCE GRAND MARNIER
POUR THESE OVER A LARGE PIECE
OF ICE IN PUNCH BOWL, THEN ADD
1/2 ORANGE AND 1/2 LEMON (BOTH
SLICED THIN), A BOTTLE OF
MARASCHINO CHERRIES, AND THE
CROWNING TOUCH — A BUNCH OF
GREEN MINT SPRINKLED WITH
POWDERED SUGAR.

FRIEND OF MY SOUL, THIS GOBLET SIP —
   'TWILL CHASE AWAY THE PENSIVE TEAR;
'TIS NOT AS SWEET AS WOMAN'S LIP,
   BUT, OH! 'TIS MORE SINCERE.

CLARET PUNCH
Good for palate and pocketbook.

1/2 POUND POWDERED SUGAR
1/2 PINT LEMON JUICE
3 QUARTS CLARET
2 QUARTS CARBONATED WATER
1 GLASS CURACAO
MIX IN PUNCH BOWL WITH A LARGE
PIECE OF ICE, DECORATE WITH FRUIT.

PINEAPPLE JULEP
For party of 6.

USE GLASS BOWL AND HALF FILL
WITH SHAVED ICE. THEN ADD:
JUICE OF 2 ORANGES
1 GILL RASPBERRY SYRUP
1 GILL MARASCHINO
1 GILL OLD TOM GIN
1 QUART SPARKLING MOSELLE
1 PINEAPPLE, PEELED, CHOPPED FINE
STIR WELL AND SERVE IN COCKTAIL
GLASSES, DRESSED WITH BERRIES.

ROMAN PUNCH
It is conducive to "roaming."

10 LEMONS (JUICE ONLY)
3 ORANGES (JUICE ONLY)
2 POUNDS SUGAR
10 WHITES OF EGGS
DISSOLVE SUGAR IN THE FRUIT
JUICES, ADD RIND OF ONE ORANGE
AND WHITES OF EGGS, WELL BEATEN.
STIR THESE THOROUGHLY, PLACE IN
PUNCH BOWL WITH LARGE PIECE OF
ICE, THEN POUR IN:
1 QUART FINE RUM
1/2 LIQUEUR GLASS ORANGE BITTERS
1 QUART CHAMPAGNE

REGENT PUNCH
Volume enough for 10, power enough for many more.

1/2 PINT WHISKEY
1/4 PINT RICH RUM
1 ORANGE, SLICED
1 LEMON, SLICED
18 LUMPS SUGAR
MIX IN PUNCH BOWL WITH PIECE
OF ICE, THEN ADD 1 PINT GREEN TEA
AND LET STAND TWO HOURS IN COLD
PLACE. ADD 1 QUART CHAMPAGNE JUST
BEFORE SERVING.

CARDINAL PUNCH
Good enough to be called the "Pope."

$1\frac{1}{2}$ POUNDS SUGAR
2 QUARTS CARBONATED WATER
2 QUARTS CLARET
1 PINT BRANDY
1 PINT RUM
1 PINT SPARKLING WHITE WINE
1 GLASS ITALIAN VERMOUTH
USE PUNCH BOWL WITH LARGE
BLOCK OF ICE, GARNISH WITH FRUIT.

POTSDAM PUNCH
Kaiser Wilhem's own.

HEAT TWO QUARTS OF WATER TO THE
BOILING POINT, ADD 4 POUNDS OF
SUGAR, THEN THE FOLLOWING:
4 BOTTLES BEST RHINE WINE
1 BOTTLE OLD RUM
HEAT THE WHOLE AGAIN TO THE
BOILING POINT, THEN TAKE FROM
FIRE AND REDUCE THE ALCOHOLIC
CONTENT BY SETTING FIRE TO THE
LIQUID. STRAIN THROUGH A CLOTH
INTO A BOWL AND ADD THE JUICE OF
TWO LEMONS. SERVE EITHER HOT OR
COLD.

(Who knows, maybe this is what started the first world war.)

HONOLULU SURPRISE
For half a dozen.

7 JIGGERS BOURBON
5 LIMES (JUICE ONLY)
3 JIGGERS PINEAPPLE JUICE
3 DASHES GREEN FRUIT COLORING
SHAKE THOROUGHLY IN ELECTRIC
MIXER WITH PLENTY OF SHAVED
ICE, STRAIN INTO SAUCER
CHAMPAGNE GLASSES.

KENTUCKY HAYRIDE
For 6 to 10.

1 PINT FINE WHISKEY
1/2 PINT FRESH CREAM
2 WHITES OF EGGS
1 TEASPOON GRENADINE
SHAKE THESE THOROUGHLY WITH
SHAVED ICE, THEN STRAIN INTO
HIGHBALL GLASSES. HALF FILL
EACH GLASS AND ADD SELTZER
UNTIL FOAM REACHES TOP.

BLACK VELVET

1 QUART GUINNESS STOUT
1 QUART CHAMPAGNE

(There is a saying that "politics makes strange bedfellows." This drink must have been political in its inspiration.)

SO LIFE'S YEAR BEGINS AND CLOSES;
    DAYS THOUGH SHORTENING STILL CAN SHINE;
WHAT THOUGH YOUTH GAVE LOVE AND ROSES;
    AGE STILL LEAVES US FRIENDS AND WINE.
                        — THOMAS MOORE

Chatham Artillery Punch
This is a whopper.

1½ GALLONS CATAWBA
½ GALLON ST. CROIX RUM
1 QUART LONDON DRY GIN
1 QUART FINE COGNAC
½ PINT BENEDICTINE
1½ QUARTS RYE
1½ GALLONS STRONG TEA
2½ POUNDS BROWN SUGAR
18 ORANGES (JUICE ONLY)
18 LEMONS (JUICE ONLY)
1 BOTTLE MARASCHINO CHERRIES
STIR ALL THESE TOGETHER AND
CHILL AT LEAST 24 HOURS. JUST
BEFORE SERVING ADD 12 BOTTLES
OF CHAMPAGNE.

*(Ought to be enough to satisfy a regiment—
from its name we gather that was its purpose.)*

Apple Punch
Will serve at least 8.

LAY SLICES OF APPLES AND
LEMONS IN ALTERNATE LAYERS IN
A CHINA BOWL, COVERING EACH
LAYER WITH POWDERED SUGAR.
WHEN BOWL IS HALF FULL POUR
1 QUART OF CLARET OVER THE
FRUIT, COVER, AND LET IT STAND
FOR SIX HOURS. STRAIN THROUGH
MUSLIN AND SERVE WITH ICE.

(An old fashioned one that listens well.)

Balaklava Nector
For a party of 12.

THINLY PEEL RIND OF ½ LEMON,
SHRED IT FINE, THEN ADD IT TO
THE FOLLOWING MIXTURE:
4 TABLESPOONS POWDERED SUGAR
1 LEMON (JUICE ONLY)
1 GALL MARASCHINO
2 BOTTLES CLARET
2 BOTTLES SODA
2 BOTTLES CHAMPAGNE
STIR WELL TOGETHER, POUR OVER
ICE IN PUNCH BOWL, DRESS WITH FRUIT

*(The name suggests the Crimea—but not a
crime.)*

I DRINK AS THE FATES ORDAIN IT.
COME, FILL IT, AND HAVE DONE WITH RHYMES;
FILL UP THE LOVELY GLASS AND DRAIN IT,
IN MEMORY OF DEAR OLD TIMES.
— THACKERY

BURGUNDY CUP
This does for about 20.

3 QUARTS BURGUNDY
1 WINEGLASS BRANDY
1 WINEGLASS RUM
2 QUARTS WHITE ROCK
1 WINEGLASS SIMPLE SYRUP
1 WINEGLASS CURACAO
1 ORANGE (CUT FINE)
1 LEMON (SLICED THIN, QUARTERED)
2 DOZ. MARASCHINO CHERRIES
MIX THOROUGHLY IN BOWL WITH ICE.
SERVE IN PUNCH CUPS.

WYNKEN
For a select few.

1 PONY COINTREAU
1 PONY BEST BRANDY
1 BOTTLE CLUB SODA
1 QUART CHAMPAGNE
1 RIND OF ORANGE (THIN)
POUR THESE OVER A CHUNK OF ICE IN
BOWL, THEN DECORATE WITH SLICED
FRESH PINEAPPLE AND ORANGE, STRAW-
BERRIES AND FRESH MIC

BLYNKEN
For a less select few.

1 WINEGLASS SHERRY
1 PONY CURACAO
1 PONY BEST BRANDY
1 BOTTLE CLUB SODA
1 QUART CLARET (OR BURGUNDY)
1 RIND OF LEMON (THIN)
1 TABLESPOON SUGAR
STIR THESE AND LET STAND FOR FEW HOURS
HOURS, THEN POUR OVER LARGE PIECE
OF ICE IN BOWL. ADORN WITH FRESH
PINEAPPLE, ORANGE AND MINT.

NOD
For JUST a few.

1 WINEGLASS SHERRY
1 PONY ANISETTE
1 PONY BEST BRANDY
1 BOTTLE CLUB SODA
1 QUART WHITE BURGUNDY
1 RIND OF LEMON (THIN)
2 TABLESPOONS POWDERED SUGAR
PUT THESE TOGETHER IN A BOWL WITH
ICE, AND GARNISH WITH SLICED FRESH
PINEAPPLE AND MINT.

ZOMBIE
Volume enough for a quartette, potency enough for the whole male chorus.

4 OUNCES PINEAPPLE JUICE
2 TEASPOONS BROWN SUGAR
2 LARGE LIMES (JUICE ONLY)
2 OUNCES LEMON JUICE
2 OUNCES LIGHT BACARDI RUM
2 OUNCES DARK BACARDI RUM
2 OUNCES HEAVY HAITIAN RUM
2 OUNCES JAMAICA RUM
2 OUNCES PORTO RICAN RUM
2 TEASPOONS GRENADINE
STIR THOROUGHLY WITH CRACKED ICE
IN A GENEROUS VESSEL, THEN DIVIDE
INTO FOUR SPECIAL ZOMBIE GLASSES.
ADD ENOUGH ICE TO ALMOST FILL EACH
GLASS, FLOAT 1 OZ. 151 PROOF DEM-
ARARA RUM ON TOP AND DECORATE WITH
SPRIGS OF MINT, SLICED PINEAPPLE
AND BOTH RED AND GREEN CHERRIES.

COFFEE ALWAYS PUTS THE FINISHING TOUCH ON A WELL PLANNED AND THOROUGHLY ENJOYED MEAL, SO IT IS FITTING THAT A FEW SPECIAL WAYS OF PREPARING THE BELOVED BEAN FOR SOME OF YOUR SWANKY SPREADS SHOULD BRING THIS "OPUS LIQUEURS" TO ITS END. HERE THEY ARE, AND WE ASK YOU TO NOTE WELL THE CAFE BRUELOT. IF YOU EVER SEE IT MADE AND SERVED AT ANTOINE'S IN NEW ORLEANS, WITH ALL THE LIGHTS OUT AND THE FLAME OF THE BURNING BRANDY ILLUMINATING THE DINERS WITH AN EERIE GLOW, YOU WILL BE CONSUMED WITH THE DESIRE TO "SPRING IT" AT YOUR NEXT BIG AFFAIR.

African Hot Punch

PLACE 4 POUNDS OF SUGAR IN A LARGE BOWL. POUR 4 BOTTLES OF BRANDY AND 2 BOTTLES OF JAMAICA RUM OVER THE SUGAR. SET THE LIQUID ON FIRE, STIR WITH A LONG METAL SPOON, THEN ADD 1 GALLON BLACK COFFEE.

Cafe Bruelot

IN A SPECIAL METAL BOWL, PLACE THESE INGREDIENTS:
2 GLASSES FINE COGNAC
4 LUMPS SUGAR
6 CLOVES
1 STICK CINNAMON
1 PIECE VANILLA BEAN
3 PIECES ORANGE PEEL
1 QUART BOILING COFFEE
STIR THESE TOGETHER, THEN PLACE BRANDY-SOAKED LUMP OF SUGAR ON SPOON AND IGNITE. CONVEY THE FLAME TO THE LIQUID IN THE BOWL AND SERVE WHILE HOT.

Cafe Royal

PUT A QUART OF HOT, BLACK COFFEE IN A METAL BOWL. PLACE FOUR LUMPS OF SUGAR IN A LARGE SPOON AND THEN POUR 2 JIGGERS BOURBON OVER SUGAR AND INTO BOWL. TOUCH A MATCH TO THE SUGAR, AND THEN IGNITE THE LIQUID IN THE BOWL. WHEN IT HAS BURNED OUT, SERVE THE COFFEE.

Cafe Grog

IN A SMALL VESSEL, PUT THE FOLLOWING INGREDIENTS:
6 LUMPS SUGAR
2 SLICES LEMON
1/2 PINT FINE RUM
1 PINT BLACK COFFEE
HEAT THIS MIXTURE UNTIL IT ALMOST BOILS, THEN ADD A PONY OF BRANDY AND SERVE.

MEASUREMENTS

1 DASH	. . . .	1/3 TEASPOON
1 BARSPOON	. . . . .	1/2 TEASPOON
1 TEASPOON	. . . . .	1 FLUID DRAM
1 TABLESPOON	. .	.1/2 FLUID OUNCE
1 PONY	. . . . . .	1 FLUID OUNCE
1 JIGGER	. . . .	.1½ FLUID OUNCES
1 WINEGLASS	. .	.2 FLUID OUNCES
1 GILL	. . . . .	. 4 FLUID OUNCES
1 PINT	. . . . .	16 FLUID OUNCES
1 QUART.	. . . .	32 FLUID OUNCES
1 "FIFTH".	. . .	25½ FLUID OUNCES

INDEX TO GLASSWARE —

BRANDY . . . . 1 OUNCE STEM GLASS

BRANDY INHALER . . . . 5, 12 AND 22 OUNCE SPECIAL

COCKTAIL . . . . 3 TO 4 OUNCE STEM GLASS

COCKTAIL, CHAMPAGNE . . . . . . 5 TO 5½ OUNCE STEM GLASS

COCKTAIL, OLD FASHIONED. . . . . 5 TO 7 OUNCE BAR GLASS

COLLINS. . . . . 10 TO 16 OUNCE BAR GLASS

CORDIALS . . . . 1 OUNCE STEM GLASS

CRUSTA . . . . CHAMPAGNE COCKTAIL STEM GLASS

DAISY. . . LARGE STEM COCKTAIL OR 6 TO 8 OUNCE BAR GLASS

EGGNOG . . . . 8 TO 12 OUNCE BAR GLASS

FIX. . . . . 8 TO 10 OUNCE BAR GLASS

FIZZ . . . . 12 OUNCE BAR GLASS

FLIP . . . . 8 TO 12 OUNCE BAR GLASS

FRAPPE . . . . 8 OUNCE BAR GLASS

HIGHBALL . . . . 6 TO 8 OUNCE BAR GLASS

JULEP. . . . . . 10 TO 12 OUNCE BAR GLASS OR SILVER CUPS

POUSSE CAFE. . . . 1 OUNCE SPECIAL POUSSE CAFE STEM GLASS

PUNCHES. . . . . 10 TO 14 OUNCE BAR GLASS

RICKEY . . . . 8 TO 10 OUNCE TALL BAR GLASS

SANGAREE . . . . 8 TO 10 OUNCE BAR GLASS

SLING. . . . . 6 TO 8 OUNCE BAR GLASS

SOURS. . . . . . 4 TO 6 OUNCE BAR GLASS OR STEM DELMONICA

TODDY. . . . . 3 TO 6 OUNCE BAR GLASS

TOM & JERRY. . . . . SPECIAL TOM & JERRY MUGS

WHISKEY. . . . . 1 TO 1½ OUNCE WHISKEY GLASS

HOT WHISKEY. . . . . 5 TO 6 OUNCE SPECIAL GLASS

WINE . . . . 1½ TO 4 OUNCE STEM GLASS

GLASSWARE CHART

Pousse - Cafe   Delmonica   Creme de Menthe   Brandy or Rum

Old Fashioned or Toddy   Whiskey   Liqueur or Cordials   Sherry

Saucer Champagne   Cocktail   Champagne Flute   Cocktail

Flip or Fizz   Punch or Highball   Tom Collins   Brandy Inhaler

POINTS TO REMEMBER—

THE PROPER USE OF ICE IS AN IMPORTANT POINT IN DRINK MIXING. WHEN SPIRITS ARE THE PRINCIPAL INGREDIENTS, USE SHAVED ICE, BUT WHEN EGGS, MILK, WINE, SELTZER OR MINERAL WATERS ARE EMPLOYED, CUBES ARE BETTER. AS A GENERAL RULE THE CUBES SHOULD BE REMOVED WHEN THE DRINKS ARE SERVED. THE EXCEPTIONS TO THIS WOULD BE HIGHBALLS AND THEIR LIKE.

SUGAR DOES NOT READILY DISSOLVE IN ALCOHOL, HENCE IT IS BEST TO DISSOLVE IT IN WATER — OR USE SYRUP.

SPIRITS SHOULD BE POURED SLOWLY INTO EGGS OR MILK, THE MIXTURE BEING STIRRED RAPIDLY AT THE TIME TO AVOID COOKING THE EGGS OR MILK BY THE ALCOHOL.

GLASSES FOR YOUR COLD DRINKS SHOULD BE CHILLED WELL IN ADVANCE.

POWDERED SUGAR IS MORE SUITABLE FOR DRINKS THAN IS GRANULATED SUGAR. NEVER USE CONFECTIONERS SUGAR IN A DRINK, SINCE IT DOES NOT DISSOLVE READILY.

WHEN MIXING A LARGE BATCH OF DRINKS IN ADVANCE, DO NOT ADD THE ICE UNTIL YOU ARE READY TO SERVE THEM. ICE STANDING IN A DRINK FOR ANY LENGTH OF TIME WILL CAUSE IT TO TASTE FLAT AND WATERY.

LEMON OR ORANGE JUICE WILL NOT KEEP PERFECTLY FRESH, EVEN IN A MODERN REFRIGERATOR. FOR BEST RESULTS, SQUEEZE YOUR JUICES AS YOU NEED THEM.

EFFERVESCENT INGREDIENTS, SUCH AS SPARKLING WINE OR CLUB SODA, SHOULD BE ADDED LAST, SO THE DRINK WILL RETAIN ITS "LIFE".

IF YOU WANT A REPUTATION FOR MIXING REALLY GOOD DRINKS, SELECT INGREDIENTS OF GOOD QUALITY. THE DIFFERENCE IN COST IS SLIGHT FOR EACH GUEST, BUT THE DIFFERENCE IN TASTE IS SURE TO BE APPRECIATED.

LASTLY, TAKE CARE ALWAYS THAT YOUR DRINKS ARE PROPERLY MADE, NEVER CARELESSLY POURED TOGETHER. USE YOUR JIGGER. GOOD DRINKS ARE NOT MADE BY GUESS-WORK.

INDEX

THESE BLANK PAGES ARE PROVIDED FOR YOUR OWN
FAVORITE RECIPES.

_____

_____

_____

_____

_____

_____

_____

_____

_____

_____

_____

_____

_____

_____

_____

_____